HOW TO BECOME EXTINCT

Will Cuppy

Illustrated by William Steig

The University of Chicago Press
Chicago and London

This edition is published by arrangement with
Holt, Rinehart and Winston, a unit of CBS Edu-
cational and Professional Publishing, a Division of
CBS, Inc.

The University of Chicago Press, Chicago 60637
The University of Chicago Press, Ltd., London

90 89 88 87 86 85 84   2 3 4 5

Library of Congress Cataloging in Publication Data

Cuppy, Will, 1884–1949.
   How to become extinct.

   Reprint. Originally published: New York:
Farrar & Rinehart, © 1941.
   1. Animals—Anecdotes, facetiae, satire, etc.
I. Title.
PN6231.A5C86   1983   814'.54   82-17649
ISBN 0-226-12826-1 (pbk.)

For Isabel Paterson
who always sees what I mean
whether I do or not

For permission to publish his little pieces in book form the author thanks *The New Yorker* and the late lamented *For Men*. Neither of these magazines had anything to do with the new and rather daring article entitled "And I Ought to Know."

CONTENTS

THOUGHTS IN THE
AQUARIUM

FISH AND DEMOCRACY

Fish are very easy to understand because only about thirteen thousand kinds or species have been discovered up to now. The term "species," in its application to fish, was first clearly defined by F. Willughby in his *Historia Piscium* (1686), and from that day to this the whole thing has been in a fearful muddle.

I ought to explain that when I use the word "fish" in this book, I may or may not mean two or more fish. In some instances "fishes" might be more correct, but in writing constantly about our finny friends one soon finds that one cannot always be saying "fishes"; one really comes to loathe oneself about the thousandth time one uses the word "fishes." It's something like using the indefinite pronoun "one" in a sentence and finding oneself stuck with it for hours at a time.

Now in Anglo-Saxon times the term "bird" or "brid" or "brydde" or some such thing meant not only what it means today, but also the young of any other animal, such as a wolf, a fox, or even a fish—or "fyshe," as they called it. And what the term "fyshe" meant, very likely, was even more foolish. You'll find none of that here. When I say fish I certainly do not mean the young of something different. I mean fish.

1

I am frequently asked: What shape is a fish? And a very intelligent question that is, too. Fish are not just any shape, as is too often the case among us higher vertebrates or non-fish. Generally speaking, fish are fusiform, or spindle-shaped, as you may readily discover by looking at a fish. The shape of a fish is more easily seen than that of some other animals. It was formerly supposed, for example, that the female members of royal families had no legs. The truth is that they have just as many legs as other people, if not more.

You have probably heard from one of your teachers that the shape of a fish is well adapted to a life in the water. Indeed, it is the chief function of the ichthyologists, or fish people, to keep pointing out, day after day, the perfect fitness of fish for existence in a liquid medium. And they're right, at that. But I sometimes think that if fish were *not* well adapted for an aquatic life—if they were square, say—then it would be time to talk.

I'm getting so I just tell people that fish live in the water and let them draw their own conclusions. If they wish to believe that fish must therefore be ideally built for a wild career on the western plains, with the Bison, that's their hard luck.

Anyway, worrying about such matters can be carried too far, as it was by old Professor Saunders, who tried to prove that almost anything dragged through a liquid medium at the end of a stout cord would in time become fusiform and fishlike, if not actually a Perch or a Flounder. He only found, after towing a large number of more or less yielding objects through the water at various speeds, that the more fragile items tended to fall to pieces and get lost after the first few miles. As fish in a state of nature do not disintegrate in this manner, or for some other reason, the Saunders expedition came to rather a loose end. In his later years Professor Saunders believed himself to be Napoleon.

I know what you're going to ask next. Can a fish hear? Well, the fish has an inner ear, or statocyst, all right, but no external auditory meatus and no membrana tympani and no Eustachian tubes—all of which leaves a bad impression. The fish people are pretty well agreed that animals cannot hear unless they have large, flapping outside ears like Elephants and the hired man on my grandmother's farm. I wonder!

In this connection, the experiments of M. Gouan of Montpellier leave us a little worse off than before. M. Gouan, who kept some

Goldfish in a vase, used to shout at them by the hour, first putting
a piece of paper in front of his mouth to prevent the vibrations

from affecting the surface, but nothing much happened; in those
days vibrations did not go through paper.

For those especially interested in the fish's sense of hearing,
there are available numerous scholarly books and pamphlets,
written in a style which is quite beyond criticism. Yet the obvious
fact that fish *do* hear—and very likely with their ears—is often over-
looked in the excitement.

I may say that I am supported in this stand by Mr. Cholmondeley-Pennell (later Mr. H. Cholmondeley-Pennell), the genial
author of some fine volumes in the Badminton Library and else-
where, inventor of the Sportsman's Travelling Hot Air Bath and
creator of the Slitless Devon Minnow—a big improvement upon
the normal Devon Minnow.

Naturally, I share this writer's views on Gudgeon fishing, a form
of sport which is (as he notes) "particularly attractive to the fair
sex," probably because you have to go out in a punt and stay all
day. I happen to know that Mr. Cholmondeley-Pennell once had
the pleasure of forfeiting a pair of gloves to a young lady who had
laid a wager that she would catch ten out of a dozen bites, "nibbles
included," and did it. She then informed him triumphantly that
her size was "sixes, sir!"

In my opinion a revival of Gudgeon fishing in the near future
would be a good joke on all concerned. Gudgeons are very greedy
and gullible. At the slightest disturbance in the water, they all

rush to the scene and are fried crisp in butter. (I wish I had time to tell you about Mr. Cholmondeley-Pennell's artificial Bleak. Anyway, he lost it the first time he tried it.)

This brings us right up against what may be called the emotional side of the fish. The popular notion that fish are mere clods is quite erroneous. Of course, they aren't Belgian Hares, but they aren't clods, either. To give you an idea: Dr. Lund shut up some male and female Perch in a box of water, and the next time he looked there were 3,215,000 baby Perch in the box, and they didn't get there by accident. I mean you don't see that sort of thing on dry land, do you?

And what, I ask you, are we to think of the viviparous fish, those that actually pair off in no uncertain manner and a little later bring forth living young! (You catch the drift?) What of the Guppyi, the Helleri, the Tetras and Danios and other tropicals with which our apartments are full to overflowing? Well, at least they keep our own offspring off the streets; you can hardly pry them away from the tank. They might miss something. I always say a small aquarium containing several of these delicately lovely creatures is truly educational, for it is here that our kiddies learn all they need to know about infanticide, homicide, uxoricide, cannibalism in the home and other familiar matters of domestic routine.

Just what these viviparous fish see in each other is a puzzle. Nobody knows exactly how and why one particular fish finally gets tied up to another fish, or which will start nagging the other one first; unless, as I am inclined to believe, it's just Fate.

Many other problems remain to be worked out by those who have nothing better to do. There are strange fish in the sea, and the general ignorance concerning them is simply amazing. What do you honestly know about the Filamentous Gurnard of the French coastal waters, the Round-headed Hassar of Demerara, or the Ginsburg's Goby of our own Chesapeake Bay, if it comes to that? Would you know a Wahoo from a Snook, or a Large-eyed Whiff from a Goggle-eyed Scad, should the necessity arise? Can you even bait your own hook? I thought so.

Yet the outlook for the future is extremely bright. (And just between you and me I think that's one of the funniest things I ever said.) The fish people are keeping at it night and day, and are able to report progress. Thanks to their efforts, we are gradually learning the real facts about the Flat-headed Chub, and as soon as we learn a few more we will all be a lot better off. By the way, the Ide is found in the Nith.

THE CARP

The Carp is dull and sluggish and greenish or brownish. You wouldn't want him around. The Carp enjoys his food because he has a peculiar palate and falciform pharyngeal teeth and a distended taste center in the hind brain. He has been called the Epicure of Fishes because he will eat anything.[1] He is fond of tallow greaves and a compost of barley meal, honey, canned corn, powdered chalk, bumblebees, cotton and cherries. Carp are rather vivacious in spring.[2] The female is friendly with three or more males and this may go on for weeks.[3] The male Carp has nuptial tubercles or warts on the face during May and June. These disappear in July and he can get something done. The senile Carp is whitish and somnolent. He doesn't know when it's June. Sometimes he can be revived with brandy.[4] There are two thousand kinds of Carplike fishes, none of them much good. The Tench or

---

[1] Strangely enough, he has also been called the Hog of the Waters.

[2] The exuberance of the Bleak at this season has won him the name of the Mad Bleak. He spawns at the age of two.

[3] Aristotle thought he had noticed thirteen or fourteen males to each female. Perhaps times have changed.

[4] One of the Carp at Versailles during the reign of Louis XIV was said to resemble Madame de Maintenon to an extraordinary degree. The story was finally traced to Madame de Montespan.

Physician or Shoemaker is coarse.[5] He lives in moats and sloughs.[6] The Gudgeon is eaten by Pike and Pickerel and people from Baltimore. The Orfe is a kind of Ide. The Zope or Swedish Bream is found in Sweden and the American Bream or Shiner is found wherever you go.[7]

[5] A live Tench applied to the nape of the neck is recommended for quartan fevers, though at some risk of hysteria.

[6] The great Tench discovered under some roots in a muddy part of the late Colonel Thornton's park at Thornville Royal, Yorkshire, in 1802, is said to have assumed the shape of the hole in which he had been confined for many years. The hole, however, seems to have been shaped very much like a Tench in the first place.

[7] A quaint old French proverb runs, "He that hath Breams in his pond is able to bid his friend welcome." And that's about all they're good for.

THE GOLDFISH

Goldfish come of a very old family, but it seems to do them no good. They have no place to go.[1] Goldfish were invented by the Early Chinese, who had little to do.[2] They have been cultivated so long that they are now useless. Goldfish have most uninteresting habits. Several times each year the males drive the females around the aquarium to teach them a lesson.[3] Queen Victoria had a Goldfish.[4] The Common or Ten Cent Goldfish has xanthochromism and cares less. He is the only kind known to some people. These people are just as well off. The Fantail is more expensive because his tail is bifid or trifid. The male Fringetail is a matter of taste. He has long floating draperies and is often petulant.[5] When en-

---

[1] The Olivaceous Goldfish of the Potomac River has succeeded in escaping from ornamental fountains in Washington. The Bar-tailed Flathead, the Large-mouthed Bass and the Common Perch do not try to escape.

[2] Much the same thing may be said of printing, which broke out in the province of Kansu in 868 A.D. The Early Chinese simply could not let well enough alone.

[3] These races provide the only clue to the sex of your Goldfish, the females invariably being the ones in front. In a small bowl, however, it is difficult to tell which one is in front.

[4] This statement is offered without documentation. It is based upon the self-evident truth that if Queen Victoria did *not* have a Goldfish, then history has no meaning and might as well stop.

[5] Goldfish quickly take on the attributes of their owners. Show me a peevish, ill-natured Goldfish and I'll show you the usual family.

raged, he flounces about, but nobody cares.[6] He is also subject to twitters.[7] He cannot help it, because he was always like that. The Japanese Lionhead or Buffalohead or Shishigashira looks very strange and probably is. Do not worry about your Goldfish. The chances are eighty-two to eighty-one that whatever you do for them will be wrong.[8]

---

[6] He particularly hates being bumped into by Tadpoles. If looks could kill there would be some dead Tadpoles in most aquaria.

[7] Cutting down on his flake food sometimes brings him to reason. If not, better trade him for something else—almost anything else.

[8] Goldfish are fond of nibbling at a bit of Anacharis, also called Waterweed or Ditchmoss or Babington's Curse. Mr. Babington had a really frightful time with it. There are nine kinds of Ludwigia in the United States. You don't need all of them.

THE MINNOW

Minnows are rather small but they are easy to get. They are found in pools, puddles, and other fishes. Minnows try to act like larger fishes, but the results are not the same.[1] They arrange themselves in circular patterns with their heads in the center. Nothing comes of this.[2] Minnows are bright and gay because they have no sense. In June they are pink underneath.[3] The Minnow can be a father but he is better for bait. He bothers the females to show that he is somebody. Minnows do not discriminate very much[4] because they are in a hurry.[5] The Killifish or Mummichog is very abundant around New York. He is full of dust and germs. The Common Killy or Salt-water Minnow is full of self-esteem. Jenkins' Killy is speckled. Lucy's Killy is not speckled. Gambusia or Top Minnows live on Mosquitoes. They are found in New Jersey. The males are only one inch long.[6] They are viviparous and both sexes are very popular. They flap a lot. Mud Minnows are found near Los Angeles. Their children are also cone-headed.[7]

---

[1] With any size of fish, there's always something. For instance, the Puffer or Blowfish grits his teeth, let alone puffing.

[2] Still, it seems important to the Minnows, nobody knows why.

[3] For this reason the Minnow is sometimes called the Pink or Penk or Cackrel.

[4] It is extremely doubtful whether Minnows can tell one another apart. And why should they?

[5] Much of the Minnow's sexual behavior may be ascribed to reflex or involuntary action. Voluntary actions are the result of thought. That is why they seem so foolish.

[6] The male appears to have no feelings of inferiority, although he is only half as large as the female. And the female knows it. She isn't blind.

[7] Some Delaware Minnows are slightly cone-headed, too. Delaware contains a good deal of poison ivy, especially around Wilmington.

THE THREE-SPINED STICKLEBACK

The Three-spined Stickleback or Prickleback or Tittlebat[1] is not much of a fish. He is only two inches long and is often found in ditches. His highest aim is to be a father and he will go to great lengths. In the spring he turns red and green[2] and builds a nest of seaweed and scraps and pushes a female Stickleback into it to lay her eggs.[3] Then he drives her away and fixes the spawn and the children never see their own mother. It's a wise Stickleback that knows anything. The father guards the nest and fans it with his pectoral fins until the children are able to shift for themselves.[4] Then he eats them. The Stickleback's home is his castle. He darts hither and thither around it, attacking larger fishes and glaring at everybody and looking very silly.[5] When swallowed by a Perch he erects his sharp spines and kills the swallower. This doesn't help the Stickleback much. He is still swallowed. The Ten-spined Stickleback has eight or nine spines. Every seven years there is a

---

[1] Or Sharpling or Banstickle or Tiddler.

[2] The older Sticklebacks do not bother to turn red and green.

[3] Female Sticklebacks associate in groups or *syngynia* until they are needed. The male Sticklebacks and the eggs are said to form a *patropaedium,* originating in a polygamous *connubium.* See?

[4] He does this because of his altruistic (parental) instinct. The higher one rises in the vertebrate scale the more altruistic one becomes. The highest vertebrates are just one mass of altruism.

[5] As some one has said, we should be poor creatures to stand up against Sticklebacks if they were as large as ourselves. But they aren't.

plague of information about Two-spined or Three-spined or Four-spined Sticklebacks.[6] This is one of the years.[7]

---

[6] Showers of Sticklebacks are sometimes reported from outlying regions. Oddly enough, these are always witnessed by the same people who see showers of Toads. For some people it is always raining Sticklebacks or Toads or Frogs or Daffodils.

[7] The Stickleback may be the Greek *Phykis,* according to Aristotle the only nest-building fish! Or the *Phykis* may have been the Black Goby or the Hake or the Wandering Chaetodon. Any way you look at it something is wrong, but there may have been a *Phykis* to begin with.

THE HERRING

Some fishes become extinct, but Herrings go on forever. Herrings spawn at all times and places and nothing will induce them to change their ways. They have no fish control.[1] Herrings congregate in schools, where they learn nothing at all. They move in vast numbers in May and October. Herrings subsist upon Copepods and Copepods subsist upon Diatoms and Diatoms just float around and reproduce.[2] Young Herrings or Sperling or Whitebait are rather cute. They have serrated abdomens. The skull of the Common or Coney Island Herring is triangular, but he would be just the same anyway.[3] Red Herrings, Kippered Herrings, and Bloaters are found in the Firth of Forth. They are eaten by peo-

---

[1] It has been figured that if the offspring of a single pair of Herrings could be permitted to multiply unmolested for twenty years, they would exhibit a bulk ten times the size of the earth. Sometimes I think that is just what has happened.

[2] Diatoms and other Plankton can be raised at home in a bowl of seawater containing a few germs. Raising microscopical objects is discouraging at first, until you get used to not seeing them.

[3] The nervous system of the Herring is fairly simple. When the Herring runs into something the stimulus is flashed to the forebrain, with or without results.

ple who eat that sort of thing.[4] Anchovies have conical snouts.[5]
Rivers from which Alewives have been driven by the construction
of dams can be restocked by placing a number of mature Alewives
above the dams. The Alewives will fall over the dams, but they
can be placed back again and again until you lose interest. The
Menhaden or Mossbunker or Pogy or Hardhead or Bughead is
nothing much.[6]

---

[4] Bloaters are held in some esteem by connoisseurs of smoked fish. But
then, connoisseurs of smoked fish are a class apart.

[5] Sprats are often substituted for Anchovies, Alewives, Whitebait, and
Sardines. You can do almost anything with a Sprat if you don't tell it.

[6] Archbishop Whately is said to have remarked that the proper female
companion for a John Dory would be Anne Chovy. That is all I know
about Archbishop Whately. That is all I need to know.

THE CODFISH

The Codfish inhabits the New England Coast and is bleak.[1] Boston is built on Codfish bones.[2] The Codfish has a sort of face because he has to have a mouth. He opens and shuts his mouth, but he never says anything. He has a barbel or cirrus on the chin and abnormal ventrals and a vacant stare, but no synovial bursa. The heart of the Codfish is made of cartilage and contains only one auricle and one ventricle. His blood is no colder than that of other fishes, it just seems colder.[3] Codfish have no vices, but their virtues are awful. The Codfish family is millions of years old and some of them look it. If you poke one with your finger and the dent remains, it is too late. He can be made into glue.[4] The head of the Codfish gradually ossifies and is fed to Cows in Norway. Codliver oil is given to disobedient children. The female Codfish lays ten million eggs but most of them never hatch. They are bet-

---

[1] The Cod must not be confused with the Bleak (pronounced Blay), so called from its pale color. The bleakness of the New England Cod is entirely a psychological affair, resulting from climatic conditions. The Newfoundland Cod is foggy.

[2] America is very rich in fishes. If we as a nation are suffering from the lack of any one thing, it is probably not fish, especially not Codfish.

[3] All fishes, of course, lack the mimetic or facial muscles so characteristic of the mammals, and are therefore unable to express their emotions above the neck. The emotions of most fishes would be difficult to express, anyway.

[4] Fish glue is used in sizing and general repair work. Nobody quite knows what sizing is. When people are asked if they wish to have some sizing done, they generally say yes. And it goes on the bill.

ter off.[5] Some fishes are brilliant in spring, but the Codfish is never brilliant. If there is a Codfish around, you know it.[6] If there are two, you move away.[7]

---

[5] The fertility of the female Cod is one of the marvels of science. One would have supposed—well, almost anything else.

[6] It has been said of this group of fishes that the Whitings speak only to Haddock and Haddock speak only to Cod. Nobody speaks to the Hake.

[7] While on a fishing excursion off Eastern Point aboard the yacht *United States* on July 22, 1873, Miss Fannie Bemis of St. Louis succeeded in capturing a Codfish weighing one hundred and thirty pounds. Miss Bemis has left no data concerning the sex of this fish. It is probable that she had no way of knowing. Possibly she would not have cared to know.

DO FISH THINK, REALLY?

This is no passing phase with me. I mean this do-fish-think problem is not something that has just occurred to me all of a sudden—something I can forget the moment I finish this piece. I only wish it were. It would be marvelous to dash off a few pages on the subject and then go ahead living my life without a care in the world, the way other people do.

No, I was always like this. Always wondering whether fish think, I mean really think. Even as a child back in Indiana, whenever I took a Butterbelly off the hook I used to ask myself, "Does this fish think?" I would even ask others, "Do you suppose this Butterbelly can think?" And all I would get in reply was a look. At the age of eighteen, I left the state.

There was nothing so extraordinary in all that, except that most children merely wonder whether it hurts the fish to get caught and yanked off a hook. And there they stop wondering, for life, apparently. No deeper levels for them. I have checked, and I find that when these children grow up their mental processes remain about the same. Does it hurt the fish? I often see people in the subway, whole rows of them, all asking themselves, as I know by the signs, that very question. Well, I'll tell them. Of course it hurts the fish. Not as much as it would hurt us to go through a similar experience, but some. Why wouldn't it?

I try not to let this fish thing dominate my life—"get me," I believe is the expression. It's been worse, though, since I heard of those Mormyrids somebody has found. Mormyrids have brains weighing from 1/82 to 1/52 of their total body weight, a proportion of brain to body hitherto regarded as impossible in a fish and, if I may say so without offense, in a great many people. Rather astonishing, eh? Well, I'm going to see that you *are* astonished, if it's the last thing I do.

Did you know that the best human brain you can find weighs only about 1/50 as much as the average human body? And that this is supposed to be tops, except in the case of certain Hummingbirds and Mice? If you have kept your eyes open, this news about Mice need not surprise you unduly. Have you ever noticed the extremely intelligent look a Mouse gives you? Ever see that look anywhere else?

In actual size and weight, of course, the human brain is outclassed only by the brains of Elephants and Whales. There is no cause for alarm here, since there are not enough Whales and Elephants to compete with us under modern conditions. Moreover, I cannot see that any useful purpose would be served by dwelling upon these statistics. As a general rule, I don't go around repeating them, and I hope you won't. Let's forget them, or try to.

Anyway, figures show that we are holding our own among the Primates, the zoological order to which we belong, scientifically speaking, together with the Apes, Monkeys, and Lemurs. The brain of the Gorilla varies in weight from 1/200 to 1/150 of its total. Our brain is therefore easily three times as large as the Gorilla's, even if we cannot crow over some of the great Ape's other dimensions.

Undoubtedly, then, we have an edge on our nearest rival in the animal kingdom, and I shall do no more than mention the other side of the picture. There are grounds for believing that the human brain is somewhat smaller than it was 25,000 years ago and I, personally, fear that the Gorilla brain is increasing in size and weight. But let's not cross that bridge till we come to it. For the present we are certainly brainier than the Gorilla, and the Gorilla seems to know it. You never hear of a Gorilla attempting mental feats for which he is totally unfitted by physiological limitations, the way some other animals do. Thus the Gorilla seldom makes a complete and utter idiot of himself, as Marmosets do so frequently.

Farther down in the scale of mammals, naturally, brains get fewer and fewer. The Beaver, smart as he is (if you think he is—I don't, myself), has a brain weighing only 1/532 of his body weight. Among the other vertebrates, the birds, reptiles, and amphibians are rated progressively lower still, with the fish almost nowhere. So wouldn't it jolt you when up pops a fish with a certified brain fraction of 1/52, almost exactly the same as *Homo sapiens*? If not, you have learned to take life's surprises with a greater degree of philosophical calm than I have, and I give you credit.

Or maybe certain fish statistics which I have had on my mind for years have left me peculiarly unprepared for the Mormyrids. It has become second nature to me, whenever I see a Pike, to exclaim, "The brain of a Pike weighs but 1/1300 as much as its entire body." Or, if it's a shark, "The Shark's brain fraction is only 1/2500, can you imagine?" I try to keep out of conversations about the Tunny, because it would seem like rubbing it in to reveal that

the Tunny's brain to body ratio is 1/3700. I know I wouldn't want that said about me.

Mr. H. Cholmondeley-Pennell, from whose delightful volume, *The Angler-Naturalist,* I learned these fish ratios, does not hesitate to draw the obvious conclusions. He sums up the Tunny in four words. "An extraordinarily stupid fish" he calls it, then drops it from his pages as unworthy of further consideration by his select readers. This judgment may be a just one, given his figures, which I have no reason to doubt. I suppose it was possible to weigh a fish quite as accurately in 1863, when *The Angler-Naturalist* was first published, as it is today.

Still, I wonder. The Tunny's reputation (or you can call it the Tuna if you prefer) has suffered ever since the Ancient Greeks began pouring out insults and errors about it by the bookful, and I don't have to tell you which Ancient Greek was the ringleader. Yes, we owe to good old Aristotle the information that the male

Tunny lacks a peculiar fin on the belly possessed by the female Tunny (he doesn't, for the female has no such fin herself), that the Tunny is wholly carnivorous (though on the next page we find it eating seaweed), that Tunnies have weak vision (but he says they see pretty well with the right eye), and that they often become so fat as to burst asunder. That isn't fat, Aristotle, it's muscle; and, by the way, Aristotle, did you ever see a bursted Tunny? They get so fat, he says, by sleeping all winter—which they do not do; if they did, would they be fatter or thinner when they awoke in the spring? (I don't know, I'm just asking.)

Aristotle, however, is correct in stating that Tunnies love to sport on the surface of the sea on moonlit nights. They do, indeed. During the full of the moon Tunnies are fools and I'm not going to try to deny it. It would be difficult, also, to explain away the unfailing regularity with which great shoals of them swim right up to the front doors of the more important canning factories at certain fixed periods of the year, just in time to be caught and pickled. There is some mental quirk here that needs attention.

The latest piece of Tunny-heckling comes from M. Le Danois, head of the Parisian Scientific and Technical Bureau of Deep-Sea Fisheries. Speaking in public on European fish conditions, M. Le Danois stated in so many words that Tunnies are unaware of the existence of the English Channel. He says that when Tunnies visit the Kattegat, Baltic, and North Seas they swim west of the British Isles, following the track used by their ancestors 100,000 years ago instead of cutting through the Channel.

You see his point. The Tunnies believe the British Isles are still part of the mainland of Europe, as they were 100,000 years ago. Naturally, they would expect to find dry land where the Channel is today, and one does not swim on dry land; so they go around. They have that much sense, anyway—eh, M. Le Danois?

Now is M. Le Danois right? He bases his theory, I dare say, upon the fact, if it is a fact, that Tunnies are never found in the English Channel; which wouldn't necessarily prove that Tunnies are unaware of its existence. I am never found in the English Channel, M. Le Danois, yet I know it exists.

Isn't it quite possible that the Tunnies go the other way simply from choice? And if this choice is influenced by their family traditions, where's the harm? I am afraid M. Le Danois is a little biased because he himself always takes to the Channel when he visits the

Kattegat, Baltic, and North Seas. And it probably never occurs to him that in so doing he is following the same path pursued by

his ancestors. That is the case, however, even if his brain does weigh 1/50 of his body weight as compared to 1/3700 for a Tunny. Frankly, on the evidence, I am compelled to doubt that M. Le Danois is actually seventy-four times as smart as the average Tunny.

Oh, well, it's probably impossible to write an article called "Do Fish Think, Really?" People like M. Le Danois and Aristotle are always bobbing up to confuse the issue and set one wondering whether the French think, whether the Ancient Greeks thought, and so forth. I could still call this piece "Do People Think, Really?" But there's no suspense in such a title. Some do and some don't. I rather fancy that statement will stand the test of time.

As for those Mormyrids that are holding up the whole problem of fish mentality with their brain-to-body fraction of 1/52, they certainly don't look it. They are only about two and a half inches long, and a couple of sillier-looking fish would be hard to find, yet there seems to be a general feeling in the scientific world that if any fish can think, *they* can. We're not likely to learn much about it, however, until the professors get good and ready to tell us. First, they must study the Mormyrids a lot more; they may even go to Africa to study more Mormyrids on their native heath. And that will be only a start. Meanwhile we must try to be patient. It may be years.

I suppose I should add that in considering the intellectual

powers of a fish one must not give undue significance to the fish's relative brain weight. The fishologists say the fish's brain-to-body weight doesn't mean so awfully much when you come right down to it, because fish have no neopallium, no matter how heavy their brains may be. That is, the thoughts of a fish with a brain ratio of 1/52 could not possibly be as worth while as the thoughts of a fishologist with the same ratio and a neopallium.

You may ask, then, why I brought up the matter at all, if it doesn't make sense. I didn't. The fishologists brought it up. They are the ones who weigh a fish and find a fraction that expresses its brain weight as compared to the weight of its entire body and stir up a big hullabaloo about it, and then tell us that it doesn't mean much of anything. That's what a neopallium will do for you.

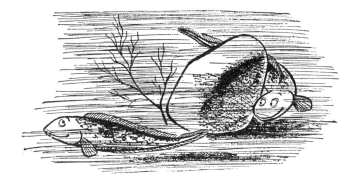

THE VIVIPAROUS BLENNY

Blennies are light-minded fishes[1] with tapering tails and a wide distribution. They might turn up anywhere. Nobody knows what to make of Blennies. Their pelvic fins are jugular and the gill membranes are attached to the isthmus. They run to fringes and filaments, but they may be found perfectly naked. Viviparous Blennies or Lumpers or Guffers or Greenbones or Eel Pouts are born already hatched because their parents were acquainted in April.[2] Infant Viviparous Blennies play hide and seek in the seaweed. Adolescent Viviparous Blennies play this and that.[3] The Shanny or British Blenny is more like a brother.[4] His head is obtusely bevelled. Palm Beach Blennies are light brown. They pounce upon Shrimps from ambush. Rock Skippers scramble up perpendicular cliffs in the East Indian Archipelago.[5] Their caudal

---

[1] That is, if one may speak of mind in this connection. The brain of the Blenny occupies but one-third of his limited skull cavity. The rest is a whitish froth resembling vanilla meringue.

[2] Blennies who bring forth their young alive, with all that this practice implies, are classified by Dr. David Starr Jordan as "degraded" forms. But for all we know they don't feel a bit that way. At least, they go right ahead.

[3] The female of any species is generally regarded as a relatively anabolic organism, more passive than the male, who is relatively katabolic and active. The fact remains that one frequently runs across a rather katabolic female.

[4] The male Shanny isn't so awfully katabolic.

[5] If you ever hear of any eccentric habit among fish, you can be sure that some species of Blenny is in on it.

peduncles are very muscular. The Common Midshipman or Singing Fish of the Pacific has luminous spots or buttons. He hums.[6]
The Pearl Fish goes whizzing in and out of Holothurians and
some day he will do it to the wrong Holothurian. Even if you have
met thousands of Blennies the next one may be worse. If some
practical use could be found for Blennies, it wouldn't help much.
Blennies simply do not matter.[7]

---

[6] See Footnote 5.

[7] Certain Blennies lay their eggs in old bottles and live there. They
are hard to find. Some people put Blennies in bottles and say they found
them.

THE SPANISH MACKEREL

The Spanish Mackerel is not especially Spanish. He has a graceful figure and is very flexible, but that doesn't make him Spanish.[1] He has a narrow peduncle and dappled sides[2] and a trilobed liver and a blue abdomen. He sounds awfully romantic but he isn't very. He is fat in the fall. What the English call the Spanish Mackerel is only the Chub Mackerel or Thimble-eye or Big-eye or Bull Mackerel. Common Mackerel are not very bright. They have no air bladders and they are caught[3] by the inhabitants of the Orkney Islands.[4] They travel in shoals because they cannot bear to be alone.[5] The sexes are almost precisely alike, but you wouldn't think so in May and June.[6] Very young Mackerel are called Spikes

---

[1] The fact is that most fishes *are* flexible when they put their minds to it. Naturally, there are exceptions.

[2] A Mackerel sky is a sky dappled with small white fleecy clouds. A Mackerel breeze is not necessarily dappled.

[3] Mackerel are often captured by jigging. Or one may drail. Drailing is also known as whiffing, railing, or plummeting. There isn't much gaffing any more.

[4] While in Greenland, Admiral Pleville-Lepley saw thousands of Mackerel with their heads sticking in the mud and their tails in the air. At least, that's what he thought he saw.

[5] The late Professor Goode believed the movements of the Mackerel to be "governed by some definite law which has not yet been worked out." The definite law is that it all depends.

[6] In Massachusetts, a startling number of Mackerel are soused from season to season.

and then Blinks and then Tinkers and then Mackerel. The Tunny or Tuna sports on the surface all night.[7] The Great Tunny has small cycloid scales. The Little Tunny has extremely small scales.

---

[7] Amphilytus the Acarnanian assured Pisistratus, before the battle of Pallene, that "the Tunnies shall dart to and fro in the moonlight." They never do anything else.

THE COMMON PERCH

The Common Perch of Europe and the British Isles is all right if you care for greenish backs and yellow sides and opalescent abdomens.[1] Common Perch go around in groups because they like to be with other Common Perch.[2] When they are alone they feel like nothing whatever.[3] Ninety-nine per cent of adult Common Perch have the minds of Minnows and Minnows have no minds at all. "You have the mind of a Perch!" is the meanest thing you can say to a fish, though the Perch themselves do not seem to resent it. They probably don't get it.[4] The American Perch or Yellow Perch or Striped Perch is about the same.[5] When it rains, he goes under bridges.[6] Perch have regular habits. If you catch one

---

[1] For some outlandish reason, Perch have teeth on the vomer.

[2] Oppian called attention to this phenomenon in his *Halieutica*, a didactic epic on fish and fishing in six books simply bulging with hexameters and other misinformation. Oppian was invented by Burton Rascoe one morning.

[3] Very young Perch occasionally associate with Pike. They do this only once.

[4] The Reverend J. G. Wood always maintained that Perch are able to communicate ideas among themselves. If so, the ideas would appear to be decidedly Perchlike.

[5] The New York Aquarium collects millions of Yellow Perch eggs in Long Island, hatches them out, and then plants them where they ought to be. Fish do not know where they ought to be. The pisciculturists hope in time to have all the fish in the right places. They already have the Walleyed Pike about where they want him.

[6] While this book was rushing to press, the New York Aquarium became extinct. It just goes to show.

of them, you generally catch the whole group, because they don't want to be different. They prefer to be caught between eight and ten in the morning and from three to six in the afternoon. If they are caught at any other time, it breaks up their day. Perch are strictly carnivorous and extremely voracious. They spend most of their time chasing and eating the smaller fish while the larger fish are chasing them for the same purpose. It does seem as though the lower animals might try to be a little kinder and stop killing each other off the way they do, life being so short and all.

THE SALMON

Salmon have strange ideas. They are afraid of parsley and slices of lemon. They reproduce only once in a lifetime, and that may be five or ten years.[1] King Salmon or Quinnat Salmon or Chinooks or Tyees travel hundreds of miles up rivers to spawn. They do this because it has always been done. The male and female pair off at the end of the journey. That is as far as they go. Salmon have adipose fins. They fix the eggs in the gravel and then they drop dead. They are not used to such things. The King Salmon has been called our noblest fish and so he is worth thirty cents a can. The Blueback or Red Salmon or Sukkegh or Sockeye is almost as noble,[2] and Cat Salmon is not noble at all.[3] Atlantic Salmon re-

[1] Generalizations of this sort must be taken in the right spirit. A few Salmon spawn two or three times. Others do nothing about it. A certain Salmon of Loch Maree was born in 1913, went to sea in 1916, and returned to spawn in 1918, 1919, 1920, 1922 and 1924. He would probably have tried again about 1927, but he was caught.

[2] All the Pacific species occur in the Columbia River, but there isn't a Blueback in the Sacramento. It's a wonder somebody doesn't put a Blueback into the Sacramento just for the fun of it.

[3] The late eloquent statesman, Charles James Fox, walking up Bond Street with an illustrious personage, laid him a wager that he would see more Cats than his companion in his walk, and that the Prince might take which side of the street he liked. When they got to the top, it was found that Mr. Fox had seen thirteen Cats and the Prince not one. The royal personage had chosen the shady side of the street as most agreeable.

turn to the sea after spawning. They do not take things so seriously. Salmon runs are twice as popular every four years. Sometimes a few immature Salmon go along just for the trip.[4] Most of
the time Salmon pursue Herrings and leap up waterfalls. When
the waterfall is too high they swim back a few yards to get a better
start. The Salmon was the first fish in the movies but not the last.

---

[4] At various successive stages Salmon are known as Alevins, Parr, Sam-
lets, or Fry (or Brandlings, Fingerlings, Skirlings, or Pinks), Smolts,
Grilse (although some Grilse are Peel), and just Salmon. After spawning,
they are Kelts or Slats or Rawners or Baggots. Sir Humphry Davy used to
speak of Grilse as "Grauls." Sir Humphry was really a sketch when you
knew him.

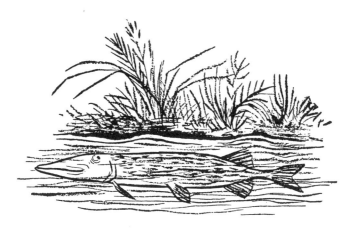

THE PIKE

The Pike is the meanest and most vicious of fresh-water fishes. This is caused by heredity and environment, or unfortunate social conditions in the water. If the other fishes would only be kind to the Pike, he would be still meaner and more vicious. The Pike has a sloping forehead and scaly cheeks and a spatulate snout.[1] He seizes his prey crosswise and swallows it headfirst. He is fond of Gudgeons,[2] Frogs, Ducks, Dabchicks, King Charles Spaniels, rubber boots, and his brothers and sisters.[3] He also attacks Horses, Mules, and Polish milkmaids, but does not get very far. Pike spawn in February, March, and April because they cannot wait until May. The females are larger but fewer.[4] The Great Middle-

---

[1] The head of a Pike, served at supper, is said to have caused the death from terror of Theodoric the Goth, who imagined the fish's features to be those of Symmachus, a man he had just killed. But for this story, we of today would have no idea what Symmachus looked like.

[2] Gudgeons are temperamental little creatures. When used as live bait for Pike, they are expected to zigzag rapidly hither and thither, but sometimes they become stubborn and refuse to budge. In a way, you can't blame them.

[3] In a singular encounter at Lord Gower's estate at Trentham, a Pike seized the head of a favorite Swan and swallowed so much of it that both perished. Lord Gower was furious.

[4] While residing at Durham, the seat of the Earl of Stamford and Warrington, the late Dr. Warwick successfully treated a female Pike for a fracture of the skull, and later reported the incident at a meeting of the Literary and Philosophical Society of Liverpool. The club members, good fellows all, roundly applauded Dr. Warwick.

Western Pike or Muskellunge is rather crude. His mouth extends from ear to ear. The Common Eastern Pickerel has fourteen to sixteen branchiostegals and that is plenty. Only one species of Pike is recognized in Great Britain. The other species are not recognized.[5]

---

[5] Boulenger unites the *Iniomi* with the *Haplomi* to form a single order. I don't, especially.

THE SLY SILURUS

The Sly Silurus or Wels or Sheatfish or European Catfish is a big, ugly fish found in the Danube and other rivers of central and eastern Europe, such as the Bug.[1] Sly Siluruses sometimes reach a length of sixteen feet and weigh four hundred pounds. As they grow older and larger around the waist, they keep on looking sly, but they fool nobody.[2] They are after Bream.[3] Because of their greed, they are easy to hook with almost any kind of bait. Which doesn't strike me as so awfully sly. Perhaps they only think they are sly. Or perhaps they are sly about the wrong things. There are no Sly Siluruses in Italy, France, Spain, or Great Britain. Some years ago, however, a gentleman reported one in the Inny, a tributary of the Shannon, the principal river of Ireland. He said he had been sitting up all night with a sick friend and had seen one on his way home along the Inny. He had jumped in after it, but it got away. Like the Common Catfish and the Mississippi Cat, the Sly Silurus is fond of muddy bottoms.[4] All Catfish are lazy, shift-

---

[1] There are two European rivers named Bug. Or there were, before all this started.

[2] Mr. H. Cholmondeley-Pennell, who probably tried it, states that "their increase with age is proportionately much more in girth than in length, and they sometimes attain such a size in the body as to exceed the compass of a man's arms."

[3] Bream seem to be fatally attracted by the six long barbels or feelers around the mouth of the Sly Silurus. You'd think a Bream would realize —or would you?

[4] The Blue Cat prefers sandy bottoms.

less and ornery. The Catfish family is not very old, dating only from the Lower Eocene. So what can you expect?[5]

---

[5] Catfish have no scales, but some of them are covered with bony plates or scutes. They are then said to be plated or scuted.

FISH OUT OF WATER

In my day it was believed that the place for a fish was in the water. A perfectly sound idea, too. If we wanted a fish, for one reason or another, we knew where to find it. And not up a tree.

For many of us, fish are still associated quite definitely with water. Speaking for myself, they always will be, though certain fish seem to feel differently about it. Indeed, we hear so much these days about the Climbing Perch, the Walking Goby, and the Galloping Eel that a word in season appears to be needed.

Times change, of course—and I only wish I could say for the better. I know all that, but you will never convince me that a fish that is out on a limb, or strolling around in vacant lots, or hiking across the country, is getting a sane, normal view of life. I would go so far as to venture that such a fish is not a fish in its right mind. There are a few fundamental truths left, thank goodness, and one of them is that a fish out of water is not where he belongs. He simply isn't.

Take the Walking Goby of Asia, Africa, and Australia, a fish with little or no respect for tradition. With the assistance of his ventral fins, he can crawl around in the mud, skip about the rocks, clamber up low shrubs, and perch upon mangrove roots. In this way he attracts a good deal of attention, and doesn't he know it?

Walking Gobies have large, protruding eyes, which they can

rotate at will. They will sit for hours on a rock, rotating their eyes, with their tails in the water, for it seems they breathe through their tails. (Oh, sure, I believe all those things.) Or a lot of them will take a long breath through their tails and go sit on a bush. To some observers, a bushful of Gobies is an inspiring sight. Others find it a little sinister.

It would be different if Gobies had to behave in this fashion. Does Ginsburg's Goby roost in the shrubbery? Or Shufeldt's Goby? Or the Fainting Goby, who wouldn't dream of so much as sticking his head out of the water? He passes out if you look at him, even. Or the Sponge-inhabiting Goby? Inhabiting sponges may be rather eccentric, I must admit, but at least it happens in the right place and not on dry land.

Another one is the Climbing Perch of the East Indies. The truth seems to be that Climbing Perch do not climb trees under their own power, not really. They are, however, frequently caught by Kites and Crows and deposited in the top branches of trees for future reference; which is not exactly the same thing—and I do hope I'm not splitting hairs again. They get very tired of their arboreal reputation, for sometimes people buy Climbing Perch and then get sore when the fish refuse to climb trees, practically accusing them of taking money under false pretenses.

The first person who reported a fish of this species climbing a tree was Lieutenant Daldorf of the Danish East India Company. While strolling near Tranquebar one sunny morning in 1791, this

young man came across what he took to be a Climbing Perch
chinning itself on the side of a palm tree, about five feet up, by
the spine of its operculum, and making every effort to ascend
higher. Six years later he published this adventure, and the scientific world went somewhat mad for the time being.

From all I can learn of his character, reading between the lines,
Lieutenant Daldorf was an upright young fellow who would not
willingly have deceived a soul. But the fact that from that day to
this, nobody else has ever seen anything of the sort, excepting the
Reverend Mr. John, a missionary residing at Tranquebar, and a
Mr. Rungasawny Moodeliar, whose story does not satisfy *me,* for
one—well, you see how it is. Those things happen.

In fairness it should be added that Climbing Perch do remain
out of water for protracted periods. They have an accessory breathing organ connected with the gills, and they probably figure that
as long as they have it they might as well use it. So they creep
around after Earthworms, hitching themselves along by means of
their pectoral fins. What is more, Climbing Perch often succeed
in tottering part of the way across the platform at fishology con-
ventions, when sufficiently prodded from behind by Tom, Dick,
and Harry. If you call that climbing a tree, well and good.

Nor are tropical fish our only offenders against what is fitting
and proper. The Common Eel has long been known, none too
favorably, for his nocturnal wanderings in fields and meadows,
where he is said to gorge himself upon green peas, his favorite
food. Ichthyologists returning from late parties have often en-
countered troops of Eels full of green peas in the dawn, scamper-
ing homeward to the nearest stream.

I have never seen Eels on dry land myself, but I am sure that
authentic instances of Eel-wandering occur. For instance, the escape of a large Eel from a tank in the London Zoological Gardens
some years ago occasioned a good deal of talk. The Eel was discovered later in another tank in a distant part of the Gardens.
Every time he was put back into the original tank he would escape
to the other one the same evening and he would be found there
the next morning. This went on for weeks. Finally the Eel was
permitted to remain permanently in the tank he so obviously pre-
ferred, and business went on very much as usual. The Eel took the
whole thing quite calmly.

The Snig or Medium-nosed Eel wanders by day instead of by
night. I haven't time to go into that now. You know where I stand.

OUR NOISIER FISH

How often have you used the expression "It sounds fishy!" without knowing what you meant by it? Do you know how a fish sounds, or haven't you the least idea? I am aware that these questions are always asked at the beginning of any article on our noisier fish. They were good enough for our grandparents, so what are you kicking about?

The fact is that fish sound very differently, depending upon the fish, and also to some extent upon the hearer or fishee. Because of peculiarities in some of the people who listen to fish, it is often difficult to establish whether a certain species may be said to bark, as in the case of the Conger Eel, or simply to buzz, bellow, or whistle.

Some people hear nothing at all when they are under water trying to hear fish. Others get a general impression of bedlam. And so it goes. Personally, when I am under water for any length of time, I get a sort of ringing in my ears. Since that occasionally happens to me on dry land, too, it probably has nothing to do with fish.

Some people, for that matter, will tell you that the Common Goldfish makes no noise, and they will try to argue the point. These are the people who say "*What* noise?" when you ask them if they were able to keep their reason while a gang of men with hammers, axes, and riveting machines were making the neighborhood a living hell all through last week. They go through life surrounded by bowls of Goldfish clucking all day and all night and they hear no clucking. Or would you say gasping? Or gulping? Or smacking? Or popping? These people would be perfectly happy under some of the subtler forms of Chinese torture. They'd never notice it.

As most of us know, to our sorrow, Goldfish come to the surface and do this whenever they take in oxygen, when they want some more flake food, when they wish the aquarium moved nearer to the window or out of a draft, when they feel like a little romp in the bathtub for a change, or just to remind you to run out and buy them another snail. My own Goldfish, or rather my last one, was hipped on the subject of heat and cold. Whenever the temperature in our apartment rose above sixty-eight degrees, he would cluck. I couldn't give in to him, for whenever the temperature falls below seventy degrees I start clucking myself. He got on my nerves, anyway. He was a Fantail.

For those who require something a little louder than a Goldfish, there is always the Growling Gourami, a fish possessing the added attraction of growling instead of clucking or gasping. This sound is described by Gourami lovers as faint but distinctly audible. It appears to be one of those things just loud enough to keep you always conscious of it and prevent you from thinking of anything else while you remain within range. It is made by the expulsion of air from the air bladder through the pneumatic duct, while Goldfish noises are made with the lips. Speaking of lips, the Kissing Gourami makes kissing motions with his all the time. Not just part of the time, but all the time. Would that appeal to you?

Perhaps the majority of noisy fishes rely for their effects upon stridulation, defined by Webster as the act or sound of stridulating, but employed by most fishologists as the act or means employed. In other words, our scaly friends produce a wide variety of sounds by the rubbing or friction of one surface of the body against another. Beginners in stridulation, such as the Ocean Sunfish, the Horse Mackerel, and the Puffer or Blowfish, attempt nothing fancier than gritting their upper and lower pharyngeal teeth.

When frightened, the Puffer or Blowfish inflates himself by gulping air until he is practically spherical, in which condition he rises to the surface and floats around on his back, helpless but safe from other fish who would like to swallow him. He is then easily captured by persons who desire to stuff him and put him on the library table. He doesn't know about us, and you can hardly blame him for gritting his teeth when he gets wise.

Other species of fish achieve more or less satisfactory results by rubbing the spines of their fins together or grinding them either in their own sockets or in the glenoid cavity. The Flying Gurnard or Sea Rooster uses his hyomandibular bone for this purpose in some manner which I haven't had time to investigate for myself and which would probably mean little or nothing to most of my readers if I had, since many of you may not even know what a hyomandibular bone is, let alone where it is and what it is good for. At any rate, the Flying Gurnard or Sea Rooster is said to crow, as the Catfish is said to purr and the Sea-horse to neigh, by people whose minds work in that particular way. I guess you have to hear those things for yourself.

Then there's the elastic spring mechanism used by the Drums, the Croakers, the Grunts, and many other noisy fish. It is a tricky form of stridulation in which modified portions of the fourth vertebra are attached to the air bladder in such a way as to cause quite an uproar under certain rather complicated conditions. The Sally Growler or Sea Raven and the Margaret Grunt are notable in this respect, not to dwell on the female Croaker, an extremely numerous type. The female Croaker has no vocal cords, but that doesn't stop her for a moment. She makes less noise than the male, but you can hear her much farther. How she accomplishes that is her own secret.

Perhaps the most interesting kind of elastic spring mechanism is that employed by the Common Crooner or Singing Fish of the California coast. You have often wondered, doubtless, how he does it, and I can't say I blame you. I've wondered myself, and I come of a musical family. It seems that he has special muscles in the walls of the air bladder, and by contracting these with almost unbelievable speed (about twenty-four times a second) he is able to throw the whole air bladder into rapid vibration, together with the gases in the various compartments of this organ. Hence the low quivering sound that some people find so depressing. The bladder itself acts as a resonator or amplifier for the constantly moving gases, which is a break for the Crooner. Without his amplifier, he would be only one more Toadfish. That's all he is anyhow.

Experiments have shown that the air bladder of the Common Crooner will continue to buzz even after it has been removed, if you stimulate its nerves and muscles with electricity. When a rubber air bladder is substituted for the real thing in the patient's interior, he appears not to mind in the least—just keeps right on crooning. If, however, the natural bladder is deflated by puncturing, the sounds abruptly cease. Too much of this sort of thing, of course, is not good for anybody. If the experiment goes on long enough, or if you lose the air bladder altogether, the Crooner has to be thrown out.

One hardly knows what to think of a fish who will go to such lengths to do something for which he is completely unequipped, even to using organs originally designed for quite other functions. Maybe the Common Crooner deserves all our sympathy and encouragement for managing to express himself against such frightful odds. I doubt it.

NOTE ON BARON CUVIER

Those who have read Baron Cuvier, the great French naturalist, may recall some of the damfool things he said about fish. The
baron possessed a really uncanny talent for guessing wrong about
the denizens of the deep, as he liked to call them. He seldom or
never missed. But one thing I can and will say for him. Although
his major premises were often terrible, he was fine on the details.

And right here is a little lesson in courage and determination.
Did the baron permit this peculiar talent to peter out from lack
of exercise? Not so you could notice it. He developed it to so remarkable a degree that he received three bushels of medals and
was finally invited to share in the government of a grateful nation.
Suffice it to say that after classifying the fish in a very odd way, indeed, he became successively Chancellor of the Imperial University, President of the Committee of the Interior, Grand Officer of
the Legion of Honor, Peer of France, and President of the Council
of State. None of which proves to me, as it does to his more rabid
admirers, that he knew his fish.

In his time Baron Cuvier said some sensible and enlightening
things about fish, too, as one can hardly help doing in the long
run, but I often think he should have stuck to his early enthusiasm
for Elephants, dead or alive, about which he wrote so charmingly,
if a trifle ecstatically, in his *Mémoires sur les espèces d'éléphants*

vivants et fossiles. You could trust the baron with an Elephant, absolutely.

With fish it was something else again. Too often, when discussing the feelings of fish, their desirability as pets, or their value as citizens, he would run on like this: "The inhabitant of the water does not attach itself. It has no language, no affection; it does not know what it is to be husband or father, or to make an abode for itself." Rubbish, Baron Cuvier!

Every single thing in that little lecture is wrong, Baron, excepting possibly the part about language, and that is extremely shaky. How do you know that fish have no language? In my opinion they have, but you wouldn't understand it because it isn't full of accents like your own. As for fish not knowing what it is to be a husband and father, where do you think Minnows come from, anyway?

And supposing a fish does not actually get married according to the rules and regulations you have in mind? Being a husband is not all of life by any means, and a French naturalist should be the last person on earth to deny it. I must say it's strange, finding you so fearfully *naïf* about one of the fundamental relations of life—for what else is there, Baron, if it comes to that?

So a fish has no affection, eh? He does not attach himself, I suppose you mean, to some particular human being and hang on to the bitter end, like the Canary and the Airedale and the people you used to know in Ashtabula. Well, I'd call that a break. Most fish, it is true, are not very responsive. You never know real trouble until you find one that is. If you want something to come lollygagging around you all the time, you're just silly to try a fish. You have to meet a fish halfway, at the very least. Three-fourths would be better.

Now, one can generally find a reason for the things people write, if one looks into it closely enough. To me it is only too evident that before launching this piece about the affections of fish, Baron Cuvier had had one or more unlucky adventures with the finny tribe and had become slightly embittered. Maybe he probed too deeply into some fish's affairs at the wrong time. I'd bet on it. Ah, well, one loves and the other loves somebody else.

In a word, you were a clever fellow, Baron Georges Léopold Chrétien Frédéric Dagobert Cuvier (1769–1832), but you were not infallible. Wasn't your Theory of Cataclysms a complete washout?

And weren't you a bit ridiculous about the Duck-billed Platypus? It is true that you were the Father of Paleontology, and by the same token I suspect that you knew a great deal more about dead and gone fish than you ever knew about fish in the here and now. As for love among the denizens of the deep, I am reluctantly forced to the conclusion that in all your life you never so much as heard of the Norway Haddock.

I may add that there is another authority whose word on this matter I would take any day before the baron's, and that is the late Mr. H. Cholmondeley-Pennell, author of *The Modern Practical Angler, Fishing Gossip,* and many other entrancing volumes, a gentleman of whose works I never tire, and a scholar whose qualities convinced me years ago that if he had not existed, it would have been necessary to invent him. This is what Mr. Cholmondeley-Pennell says:

> Under certain circumstances fish have been known to exhibit a very decided affection for members both of their own and of other species. Such affection, however, has been most commonly observed to exist between fishes of the same species, but of opposite sexes, at the time of spawning.

It is really too bad, Baron, that you never read the works of Mr. H. Cholmondeley-Pennell. There was a man who had lived.

REPTILES I'M ALWAYS MEETING

OWN YOUR OWN SNAKE

Snakes are vertebrates and the vertebrates are classified as higher animals, whether you like it or not. I mean you can be a higher animal and still be a snake. This seems a rather peculiar arrangement, to be sure. If you can think of a better, let's have it.

Snakes affect different persons in different ways. Some loathe snakes so much that they won't even read about them—and you ought to know some of these people! Others actually love snakes. Which brings us rather neatly to the first main subject or theme of this article: the snake as something to love. (I see the weakness of this theme as well as you do. The snake is *not* something to love.)

Do you know how many people in this country keep snakes as pets? I thought not. Even more people, of course, do nothing of the sort, and most of these would condemn the practice as morbid or worse. Frankly, considering what some of them do pet, I don't see why they should draw the line at snakes.

My own attitude is pretty tolerant. I don't care what people do about anything, let alone what they do about snakes. I may add

47

that in my own case the problem of loving a snake or not loving a snake has never come up. I may be the type that just doesn't care to have a houseful of snakes for my very own. If I were crazy about snakes, I'd have some, wouldn't I? Or maybe I haven't met the right snake.

There are many arguments, none of them awfully good, for having a snake in the house. There's the familiar one that a snake is better than nothing. Well, that hasn't a leg to stand on, if my experience with a certain pet—a non-snake—is any criterion. Never take up with an animal that is merely better than nothing. Some day you may thank me for this tip.

I'd like to give a little advice to those who keep poisonous serpents around, but life has taught me that such people do not take advice. I had that out with a lady correspondent who used to write me about her pet Rattlesnakes and other diabolical species. Every time she got a new Fer-de-Lance or a Bushmaster, she would write and tell me what a darling the fellow was, knowing only too well that I wouldn't sleep a wink that night. She knew I would sit up and answer her letter, urging her to be more careful with the deadlier varieties.

One of this lady's contentions was that snakes are fundamentally friendly creatures, seeking only to be pals with those whom Fate has cast in their way. Snakes do not want to bite you, she said, they much prefer not to bite you. She was so tiresome on this point that I watched for a chance to get even, and finally it came. One of her letters contained the statement, "Snakes never bite unless they are frightened." I immediately sent her the following note: "All right, then, snakes never bite unless they are frightened." Brief but to the point, eh?

I lost track of the lady a couple of years ago, so I can't give you her latest opinions. Perhaps she got tired of my constant warnings. Her last letter, though, was as long and chatty as ever, all about the gigantic King Cobra she had acquired from the jungles of Malaysia. He was a perfect dear, she said, and just loved to be chucked under the chin with the petting stick. (The petting stick is a stick padded at the end, with which snake lovers stroke and tickle the objects of their affection, mostly from a safe distance. And how would *you* like it?) The very next day, I recall, she was going to enter the King Cobra's cage and give it a good tidying up.

Among the harmless ophidians, the Gopher Snake is a favorite pet with many. It grows as long as nine feet and it hisses loudly most of the time, but you could get used to that. This snake is just what you want if you suffer from Pocket Gophers, as a great many people do, surprising as it may seem in this day and age. How little we know about the lives of our own fellow creatures, when you come right down to it. But, my God, Pocket Gophers!

"Do snakes make intelligent pets?" and "How intelligent is a snake?" are questions I am often asked, sometimes by people you wouldn't expect to bring up the subject. I generally tell them how the big Boa at the London Zoological Gardens swallowed her blanket, first constricting or squeezing it in the approved manner, apparently in the belief that it was a live goat. This little anecdote invariably disappoints all who hear it. They seem to think it should be longer, or funnier. Why is it that people don't see the significance of things any more? Is it a trend?

Some snakes are intelligent enough, if you don't expect much. Others aren't. I hesitate to speak of Butler's Garter Snake in this connection, for even the simplest statistic about it sounds insulting. Its head is only five-sixteenths of an inch wide, or about half what a Garter Snake's head should be. It is pretty clear that nothing of any importance could happen in such a head; though, for all I know, they may think they're frightfully clever. Butler's Garter Snake gets by, that's about all you can say.

Butler's Garter Snake inhabits Ohio and Indiana, also parts of Michigan, Wisconsin, Iowa, Kansas, and Nebraska. Observers who report it from western New York and Pennsylvania are probably Middle Westerners trying to be nasty. A related species is the Narrow-headed Garter Snake of California, a state in which several kinds of reptiles are noted for their limited cranial capacity. Scientists do not know why this condition should exist in only one particular region, but I know. Mother Nature just thought more head would be a waste of material.

Here is the place, by the way, to mention those herpetologists who specialize in Garter Snakes. Herpetologists are people who know all about snakes and other reptiles, also amphibians. They are like other people, except that they are herpetologists. By counting the dorsal scales and the labial, ventral and subcaudal scutes, studying the stripes, and measuring the tails of thousands and thousands of Garter Snakes, they have succeeded in dividing the little fellows into a number of species and subspecies; more, to be candid, than actually exist. For each new species he discovers, the herpetologist receives a bonus. Would that explain it?

Yet herpetologists have their place in the scheme of things. Because of them, we know that Butler's Garter Snake has, in most instances, only six supralabials, a state of affairs caused by the fusion of the penultimate and antepenultimate scutes. We who take our Garter Snakes so lightly may well give a thought to the herpetologists counting scutes on the genus *Thamnophis* in museum basements while we are out living our lives. Most of the specimens are pickled.

No article entitled "Own Your Own Snake" would be complete without a glance at Aristotle, with whom I have been conducting a feud on problems of natural history for some years now. And so far the odds are in my favor, if I do say it. I ask little credit for my victories over the Father of Learning, as they call him. They're too easy. Every time I look up something in his works, darned if the old boy isn't screwy. I suppose the rest of his stuff is fine. I just happened to look at the worst places.

Take the snake's tongue, perhaps the most controversial subject in herpetology. What says the old Stagirite? (That's what he was, you know.) Turn to Line 5, Section 660ª, of *De Partibus Animalium* (Oxford, 1912), and read that this organ "is forked and has a fine and hairlike extremity, because of their [serpents'] great liking for dainty food. For by this arrangement they derive a twofold pleasure from savours, their gustatory sensation being as it were doubled."

Well, that's the way it goes in this business. You save up a reference for years in order to convict a rival of feeble-mindedness out of his own mouth, and when you come to use it, the thing has evaporated somehow. I would have sworn that was the silliest quotation I ever saw in my life, and I've seen plenty.

Aristotle's view of the snake's tongue, somewhat in eclipse during the Dark Ages, when people had no time for such foolishness, came to the fore again with the Revival of Letters and held first place in the schools until shortly before the Repeal of the Corn Laws. During that entire period, as today, there was a strong popular suspicion that the snake bites, or stings, with the tongue, squirting the venom through the flickering filaments and injecting it in some unknown manner with the same instrument, though where that would leave the teeth and fangs it would be hard to say. The last scientist of any eminence to support this view was a Dr. W. Holt Yates, M.R.C.P., President of the Royal Medical Society of Edinburgh, and author of a *History of Egypt*. Nobody, including his immediate family, took Dr. Yates very seriously.

We of the Lost Generation were taught that the snake hears, as well as feels, with the tongue. It sounded silly, but we took it, doped as we all were by World War I, or were we just naturally dopes? As we rush to press, the latest snake book tells us that snakes do not hear with the tongue at all—they *smell* with it, for Godsakes. A snake can smell with its nose if it wants to. It can also smell by darting out its tongue and then sticking it up into its Jacobson's organ in the roof of its mouth. Working frantically back to the fountain-head, I find that Dr. Ditmars himself, in his *Snakes of the World,* says the snake's tongue enables it "to detect vibrations and to instantaneously 'taste' various odors either in the air or on the ground." Are you still with us?

Do you see what this makes me, when I practically called Aristotle a halfwit for saying that snakes smell with their tongues? Do you get the full force of it? Let this be a lesson to all authors who are trying to prove something. Don't make up your piece as you go along, trusting that your authorities will say what you thought they would say. First get your facts, and then write your piece, if write you must. As for Aristotle, I'll get him the next time. Father of Learning, my eye!

But speaking of sex, pet snakes are disappointing. They are not in the mood, apparently. Snakes are at their best in a wild state, where conditions are free and easy, to say the least. As Darwin puts it in *The Descent of Man,* "Male snakes, though appearing so sluggish, are amorous." Isn't that just like Darwin? It was one of his main ideas, you know, that the males of almost all animals have stronger passions than the females. Since then we've learned a thing or two. At any rate, the female snake is right there when spring arrives in the woods.

The social life of the snake, I fear, is not all that might be desired. Dr. Ditmars, who is no alarmist, says that Rattlesnakes, Copperheads, and Blacksnakes mate as soon as they emerge from their dens in May, even before they take a bite of food, which shows only too plainly which way their minds run. Snakes are born in summer, and it is believed that most of them mate during their second or third spring, that is, at the age of a year and a half or two years and a half. They figure they're only young once.

You have to follow a snake around before you know it. DeKay's Snake always struck me as a quiet and well-behaved sort until I learned some of its habits. It mates at the age of eighteen months. You'd expect that of the Striped Swamp Snake, but hardly of DeKay's. And I suppose there's no use trying to hush up John's Sea Snake, which mates when only *six* months old. At that age both the male and the female John's Sea Snake are sexually mature, and I don't mean maybe.

Snakes, in a word, are well worth knowing, unless you'd rather know something else. In closing, I have a little message which I wish you'd relay to some of those people who won't read a snake article because it gives them the jumps: There are no snakes in Iceland, Ireland, or New Zealand. And no snake articles.

THE GARTER SNAKE

The Garter Snake or Striped Snake is our most abundant North American serpent.[1] Although they are always getting killed or driven from their natural homes, there are just as many Garter Snakes as ever, and I can tell you the reason.[2] Garter Snakes are crazy about sex and they don't care who knows it. On a warm day in spring several hundred Garter Snakes may be seen all heaped together in a large squirming bunch, or bundle, with their heads sticking up in the air. If you throw a stone at them they will glare at you and hiss, as who wouldn't? This is called bundling, or squirming in bunches. It doesn't look like much fun to us humans, but the Garter Snakes go right on doing it every spring.[3] Snake professors of the old school said little about this habit, hoping Garter Snakes would outgrow it, but they didn't. The modern Garter Snakes are worse, if anything.[4] Garter Snakes have enor-

---

[1] It is called the Garter Snake because it had to be called something.

[2] It is almost impossible to keep Garter Snakes out of city parks. They multiply faster than park policemen.

[3] In 1878 Dr. E. Coues noticed a small group of Garters bundling as late as October. In any species you'll always find a few members who overdo it.

[4] Extremely old Garter Snakes generally stay out of these bunches. Still, they have their memories.

mous families. Some females give birth to eighty-five children at once. If you do this year after year, it soon counts up.[5] As soon as they are born, young Garter Snakes crawl away in search of Earthworms.[6] Some people say the mother Garter Snake swallows her young when danger threatens, disgorging them later, and they stick to their story through thick and thin. They feel that they simply couldn't go on unless Garter Snakes swallow their young, and if you deny it they will write to you and tell you that you are a heel. I am often asked, "What do Garter Snakes think about?" They think about sex and Earthworms. Others inquire, "What are Garter Snakes good for, anyway?" There is no answer to that.

---

[5] Several years ago a Garter Snake at the Bruce Museum became a mother twice in the same week, having sixty-three babies in all. It caused a good deal of talk around Stamford, Connecticut.

[6] Garter Snakes are born in August, making them either Leo or Virgo characters.

THE COMMON VIPER

The Common Viper is found in most parts of Europe.[1] He lives largely upon Rats, and Europe is full of Rats. The Common Viper frequents dry, sunny spots, haystacks, old barns, nudist colonies, or any place where you would like to sit down and have a picnic. The bite of this snake seldom kills you. It only makes you awfully sick and ruins your vacation. Vipers are very sociable among themselves. They come out in the spring to wiggle around and get acquainted with each other, and the young are born alive four months later.[2] Young Vipers are just as mean as their mothers and almost as poisonous. Baby Vipers that bite somebody right away are regarded as promising children. Vipers hiss at everybody who doesn't belong to their family. They hate their own family, but they hate outsiders even more.[3] Common Vipers are easy to spot, as they are gray, greenish, yellowish brown, reddish, or black. There are plenty of other Vipers if you know where to look.[4] The Puff Adder and the Rhinoceros Viper of Africa should not be allowed. They hide in the sand and bite you in the foot. The Gaboon Viper bites you in the Gaboon and then waits around to see

---

[1] We have no Common Vipers in the United States, but we have worse.

[2] It's a wise Viper that knows his own father. Among the Vipers, life is not like that.

[3] The Supercilious Viper is found in Mozambique, of all places in the world to be supercilious in!

[4] If you go around handling Vipers, perhaps the best kind to handle would be Orsini's Viper, a Central European species. He has poison fangs, but he seldom bites. Hardly ever.

how you like it.[5] Vipers attain their growth in about seven years and they get nastier every day. Vipers show what Mother Nature can think up when she puts her mind to it. If you want to be kind to Vipers, that is your privilege. I'm only telling you.[6]

---

[5] Even Dr. Ditmars doesn't care for Gaboon Vipers.

[6] Pliny the Elder states that Vipers are not venomous when asleep. That is called classical learning.

THE RATTLESNAKE

Other countries may boast of this and that, but nobody can touch the United States for poisonous snakes. We have about twenty species, most of them deadly, and Europe has only five or six, none of them much good. We have fifteen kinds of Rattlesnakes alone and nobody else has even one.[1] Rattlesnakes inhabit every state in our nation except Maine, Vermont, and New Hampshire, which are peculiar, anyway.[2] The Diamond-back Rattlers of the South are six to eight feet long and twelve inches around the waist. Other places have to be satisfied with smaller ones. The Timber or Banded Rattler of the East is only four or five feet long. The Pygmy Rattler is so small that he seems just silly until he gets you. Rattlesnakes are Vipers, but not True Vipers. They are Pit Vipers because they have pits or cavities between the eye and the nose.[3] Ophiologists, or snake experts, do not know why Pit Vipers have pits. They have pits so that we can tell them from True Vipers. Rattlesnakes spend the winter in a torpid condition in their dens, huddled together or entwined. This is worth mentioning, as most animals are not torpid when they are entwined.[4] Young Rattlers begin their social life at the age of two years, long before they are grown. If they waited until they were grown, they

---

[1] There is a species in Central and South America, but it probably came from here.

[2] There are none in Long Island, thank God.

[3] The Jumping Viper, or Mano de Piedra, of Central America, is a Pit Viper. As he leaves the ground when striking, you never know where you are.

[4] A few animals appear to be torpid all the time.

might miss something.[5] Most Rattlesnakes rattle before they strike, but some do not, which is a good thing to know. Some people think the Rattlesnake is very kind and noble, and rattles so that we will run away and not get bitten. Others think it is just a form of meanness.[6] Ophiologists insist that the Rattlesnake renders services to mankind, such as eating rodents, and is thus of economic value. If I want any services rendered, I'll get somebody else. When you hunt Rattlesnakes, be sure to take along some high shoes, a pair of leather puttees and, if possible, Dr. Ditmars.

---

[5] Rattlesnakes get along together all right. There's no accounting for tastes.

[6] Rattlers never bite unless they are offended, and they are offended rather easily, considering the fact that they're only snakes.

THE BOA CONSTRICTOR

The Boa Constrictor of Central and South America belongs to the family *Boidae,* and what a family![1] Like the Anaconda and the Python, much larger snakes of the same family, the Boa Constrictor squeezes his prey before swallowing it whole.[2] The Boa Constrictor is only twelve or fifteen feet long, so he could hardly swallow a man, although he could squeeze you slightly out of shape. He could only swallow you as far as your shoulders, but you would still have the worst of it because of the wear and tear.[3] The Boa Constrictor does not break your bones, except some of the smaller ones, maybe. He just squeezes you enough to make you stop breathing.[4] Besides, he doesn't do this from evil motives.

---

[1] Herpetologists have recently decided that the Boa Constrictor should be called *Constrictor constrictor.* I have decided that it should not. Two can play at the game.

[2] All the *Boidae* constrict, or squeeze, but they don't really love you.

[3] He is not poisonous, if that helps any.

[4] Nervousness probably plays a part in this. Some people go all to pieces when squeezed by a snake.

The poor thing is hungry. Boa Constrictors become very tame in captivity. If your Boa starts to constrict you, catch hold of his tail and unwind it, at the same time yelling, "Help! Murder!" Then take up some other hobby. The Anaconda or Water Boa of South America is about thirty feet long. If he pursues you while you are in swimming, he probably thinks you are a young Tapir.[5] Your best move is to swim for the shore, hoping he will not come up from below and bite you, as he often does. His teeth are almost two inches long.[6] Pythons are even larger than Anacondas and they swallow larger animals. They live in India, Malaysia, and Africa. You can avoid Pythons by keeping out of such places.[7] Pythons are oviparous. The female Python often sits on infertile eggs. She doesn't know that eggs have to be fertilized before they will hatch. She's funny that way.

---

[5] It is surprising how many people resemble Tapirs when you get a good look at them.

[6] Then you might climb a tree. Anacondas also climb trees.

[7] Pythons think nothing of going six months without food. They are waiting for something worth while.

THE COBRA

We should always be kind to every living thing, excepting maybe the Cobra-de-Capello. The Hindoos are kind to the Cobra because it is against their religion to kill him. So every year he bites from five to ten thousand Hindoos and that is the last of *them*.[1] The Cobra is not civilized. He bites whenever he is angry, and he gets angry if you only step on him or poke him in the eye. If he were more civilized, he would try to make friends before biting you. Unlike most snakes, the Cobra sits up on his tail, expands his hood and strikes, then holds on and chews you for a while so that there will be no mistake. Your only chance with a Cobra is to grasp him by the neck, but there is a trick in this and you should take a few lessons in Cobra-grasping before you begin.[2] The Mongoose dashes at the Cobra repeatedly until it tires out the snake and the whole movie audience. Cobras are supposed to dance to the sound of the Hindoo flute, but they are only swaying with the flutist to get into biting position. They cannot hear the flute, lucky fellows! In family affairs the Cobra is just folks. At certain seasons the female may be seen in the woods with two or three males. They are out picking daisies.[3] The female Cobra sits on her eggs so that the children will all hatch out and grow up to be like father. The King Cobra or Hamadryad is eighteen

---

[1] A few Cobras in your home will soon clear it of Rats and Mice. Of course you will still have the Cobras.

[2] When held up by the tail the Cobra cannot bend his head back enough to bite your hand. That wouldn't prevent his getting you on the uptake.

[3] The Cobra has a rather remarkable hypopallium—that is, for a snake.

feet long and as mean as they come. He is said to be very intelligent because he recognizes his keeper at the Zoo and comes out of his corner for food. I don't call that so intelligent. I could do it myself.

THE HOG-NOSED SNAKE

The Hog-nosed Snake is a brownish little fellow about as big around as your thumb.[1] He operates back of the beaches in Long Island and New Jersey, where there are plenty of Hoppy Toads and fresh air, and he could lead an ideal life if he had any sense. He is perfectly harmless, but he pretends to be a deadly African Puff Adder. Then he wonders why people kill him.[2] When he sees you the Hog-nosed Snake flattens his head and neck, swells up his body, sticks out his tongue and hisses like the worst of the Vipers. This may frighten a few timid observers, but we insiders know it is all a bluff. Personally, I think nothing of picking one up on the end of a long stick and throwing him around.[3] If you annoy the Hog-nosed Snake enough, he will roll over on his back and play dead. If you then turn him right side up, he will roll over again to prove he is dead.[4] You see he's quite hopeless, mentally. He hasn't thought the thing out. He can't. Many people who know

---

[1] As his nose turns up a trifle, he was once called the Buckwheat Nose. I don't quite get it myself.

[2] Most people erroneously call this snake the Puff Adder, Beach Adder, or Blowing Viper. So, naturally, they kill it.

[3] There is always a catch in pretending to be so tough. You may meet somebody who actually *is* tough.

[4] While he is playing dead, you can go straight up to him and step on his head or smash him with a big club.

that the Hog-nosed Snake is harmless will kill him anyhow, and you can hardly blame them. They figure that after all a snake is a snake.[5] Besides, when dealing with a Hog-nosed Snake one always has a feeling that this particular snake may be a Copperhead on a weekend visit from upstate or a Puff Adder which somebody has brought over from Africa and mislaid, and one seldom has time to hunt up an ophiologist and ask him about it. Before the situation can be improved we must either educate the snake or educate the public, but both of these plans have been tried.

---

[5] Unfortunately there is a grain of truth in this theory that a snake is a snake—just enough to put one off.

ARISTOTLE, INDEED!

I have received a curious letter from a lady who signs herself "Furious." The communication reads in part:

> I guess you think you know it all, don't you, Mr. Cuppy? I have admired some of your articles. I loved the one about the Yak. [Author's note: I have never written an article about the Yak.] But when you attack Aristotle, the greatest thinker who ever lived, like you did in a piece entitled "Own Your Own Snake," you are out of your depth. Aristotle had more sense in his little finger than you have in your whole ugly carcase.

Sez you! I may be dumb, "Furious," but you're not putting anything over on me with that letter, not for one moment. I know what you mean, for all your beating about the bush and saying you admire me and all that. You mean I am not as smart as Aristotle, and you needn't try to deny it. I can read between the lines as well as the next one.

I'll give you credit for one thing, "Furious." You have raised an issue that will have to be met sometime, sooner or later. I was hoping it would be later. Whether Aristotle was a smarter man than I am, or vice versa, is a point, however, to be determined by a group of duly constituted authorities, not by some flighty young woman in a pet. Do you follow?

And while I'm about it, I may as well add that your use of the word "like" in the expression "like you did" is not English. The word you were groping for is "as." "As you like"—see? I suggest, for your own good, that you spend part of your time each day learning the language. Or why don't you take up tatting? You might have a future there.

It's very strange, too, your leaping to the defense of an ancient Greek who died in 322 B.C., as if he were your best friend in an awful spot and only you could save him. There's something back of this, "Furious." Have you got Aristotle mixed up with some other old Greek you happen to have met around town? Are you barking up the wrong Greek? Or is it just some personal grudge you have against me? A member of the Hate Cuppy Movement, eh?

The fact is, I gave Aristotle quite a break in that article. I only quoted a sentence or two from his study of the snake's tongue and made a few remarks—disparaging, it is true, but nothing to what he had coming. Is it my fault if anything one quotes from Aristotle sounds as if he was a little touched in the head? And does that necessarily make him the greatest thinker of all time?

I don't doubt that Aristotle thought more in actual footage during his life than any other person ever thought in the same elapsed time of sixty-two years. I do say, however, that any prize he deserves for so doing should be for quantity, not quality, as a great deal of it was spinach. He would sit around and think like one possessed, or he would walk around and think, since he was a Peripatetic, as they called it in those days. And then he would announce that Swallows spend the winter under water on the bottom of ponds and streams, or that Eels are the product of spontaneous generation, or that women have fewer teeth than men. And then it would be published and taught in the schools, because it sounded like the sort of thing that always *is* taught in the schools.

Still and all, Aristotle stimulates you. He keeps you guessing, not only about what he meant but about what he thought he meant. Take what he says about the snake's legs—or lack of legs, rather. He says snakes have no legs because, if they had any, they would have only two or four, and that wouldn't be nearly enough. You can stay up all night figuring that one, snatch a few winks of sleep, and fly at it again the next morning. And you'll be little the wiser. All you'll be is a wreck.

How, you may wonder, did Aristotle arrive at this goofy bit of natural history? Well, he had a theory that "no sanguineous creature [by which he meant red-blooded] can move itself at more than four points." "Granting this," says he, and I'll grant it, merely to see what happens—"Granting this, it is evident that sanguineous animals like snakes, whose length is out of all proportion to the rest of their dimensions, cannot possibly have limbs; for they cannot have more than four (or they would be bloodless), and if they had two or four they would be practically stationary; so slow and unprofitable would their movement necessarily be."

Now that's what I call talking too much. That particular passage has taken so much out of me that I can't go into it and parse it the way I should. But I can see what it's driving at. Snakes have no legs because it wouldn't jibe with a rule that Aristotle made up himself out of his own head—that stuff about the four points. And if they had two or four legs, they would be rooted to the earth, as

if they were nailed down. Honestly, if *I* made a practice of promulgating such drivel, where would I be today? In Ward 8.

Of course, there's always the chance, however slim, that Aristotle may know what he's talking about. Some rather long lizards have only four legs. Maybe they can't have any more. Maybe they do have only four places where they can have legs. Even so, they seem to get by with the four. They aren't stationary. Then why couldn't a snake get along with only four legs, too? Surely four legs are better than none. And then again, snakes abandoned legs during the course of evolution. They thought it all over for millions of years and they don't want any legs. You have to consider that, too.

It is a pity that Aristotle didn't drop the whole subject with the comment he made in another place: "Serpents, like fish, are devoid of feet." There is a statement worthy of a scientist. I couldn't improve on it myself. It says nothing about legs, but the implication is clear, for nobody would expect any legs where there are no feet. It is not brilliant, but it is true, and true it will remain until Dr. William Beebe shows up at the American Museum of Natural History with a four-footed fish, which might be any day now.

In a word, Aristotle's discovery that snakes and fish have no feet is a keen bit of observation for an ancient Greek, but why should it make him the Father of Learning?

Yet there is something else about the snake that our old friend missed altogether. He said snakes do not have something which they certainly do have, for when snakes were deciding what to abandon as they evolved, they appear to have voted unanimously to keep that one, though the heavens fall, and they have stuck to it through thick and thin. Snakes have a pretty firm grasp of fundamentals when you come right down to it, and a fine feeling for what is essential to life, liberty, and the pursuit of happiness. Snakes are perfectly O.K. in that way.

You may wonder how Aristotle could make such an error, when the subject was right up his alley. He had what amounted to a yen for investigating the more recondite anatomy and watching the private gyrations of even the humblest creatures, so much so that one wonders how he ever found time for his own dates. Well, he appears to have convinced himself by the use of pure reason that snakes would not be any fun to watch because they were footless animals, and he had already laid down a certain rule about the way footless animals were built. This teaches us that the thing to do is to look at the animal.

Aristotle, of course, was frequently right, for it is almost impossible, under the laws of chance, to be wrong all the time. Thanks to him we know that the Weasel does not bring forth its young by the mouth, as held by Anaxagoras. He also denied that Hyenas change their sex every year. He was only guessing, but it sounds like a good guess. I don't know what to say of his theory that flat-footed people are treacherous. Some of them are, very likely.

If Aristotle could speak for himself, though, he would probably tell us that he never wrote half the tosh they call his, at least in its present form. His books may be only lecture notes taken down in class by some of his backward pupils and later touched up from time to time by professors of philosophy. Have you ever met one of those?

Also, after everything has been done that can be done, the commentators are always having to explain that part of this or that sentence must have been lost in transit. It dropped out some way, that's why it doesn't make sense. That's fine for Aristotle. I only wish a few commentators would get busy with my works and tell the public it isn't my fault. Part of it must have dropped out when I wasn't looking. Or some fiend broke into my office and garbled the manuscript before I could send it off to the publishers. I have never seen any of these manuscript garblers myself, but perhaps they exist.

Anyway, Aristotle should worry. I was glad to see, when I called there recently, that the reference department of that splendid institution, the New York Public Library, contains enough index cards on Aristotle to choke a herd of Elephants, all referring to several miles of the actual volumes in the stacks. Swell! Give our growing citizens plenty of Aristotle, and you'll have a lot of citizens who have tried to read Aristotle.

I haven't a spark of envy in my whole system, but I couldn't help noticing, as I just happened to be riffling through the files, that they haven't so much as one card on any of *my* books. Not a mention, not a whisper, about a single one of the Cuppy volumes, all two of them. They don't take me seriously, I suppose.

I'm not kicking. I'm only hinting that Aristotle never had anything like that to contend with. All the libraries in the world have been buying his books like mad for two thousand years, and they would buy more if there were any more. Naturally, with that kind of help, his fame is now so secure that you can't budge it. I can't honestly feel that I've budged it an inch, pick on him as I may, year in and year out.

Well, I've always said, and I say it again, I ought to be more of a mixer. I guess I don't get drunk with the right people.

THE GLASS SNAKE

The Glass Snake is something else again. He looks exactly like a snake, and everybody calls him a snake, and for two cents I'd call him a snake myself. But he is a lizard because, to begin with, he has movable eyelids and his abdomen is a little different.[1] Besides, no snakes have any trace of the pelvic girdle,[2] while no limbless lizards—or, rather—can't you just take my word for it?[3] The Glass Snake is famous for snapping off his long tail when closely pursued or otherwise frightened.[4] The tail jumps and thrashes around on the ground like another animal to distract the enemy's attention, permitting the front end to escape and grow a new tail. This sounds like more fun than it really is, for the Glass Snake can do it only once and the new tail isn't nearly as good as the old one.[5] The Glass Snake should think twice before he snaps off his nice long tail. His head is only five-eighths of an inch wide, however, and he does very well to think once. Therefore many Glass

---

[1] For the facts about the Glass Snake's abdomen you'd better see a professor. I'm busy now.

[2] Except a few species, which *have*.

[3] I always say you can't be much of an animal without a pelvis. Want to make something of it?

[4] Well, that's one way of getting famous. I'd call it the hard way.

[5] Glass Snakes do not go back later and patch the front end on to the old tail, no matter what your Uncle Jim says. I know he's *seen* them, but forget it.

Snakes lose their tails before they have seen life. You could explain all this to the young Glass Snakes, but you would be wasting
your time. They have to live and learn.[6] In captivity, a pair of
Glass Snakes are happy enough if left to their own devices, of
which they seem to have several. But being so breakable must
make them awfully nervous. I know it would me.

---

[6] Maybe they don't care about their tails, anyway. I don't know. I'm
not a Glass Snake.

THE CHAMELEON

Speaking of lizards, the Chameleon is one of the oddest.[1] Florida or Pet Chameleons are not really Chameleons, though they will do in a pinch.[2] They can be taught to run up your leg and that sort of thing and they often stop biting you after a week or two. The real or Common Chameleon lives in trees in northern Africa and such places. He spends his day rolling his eyes, catching Flies with his long sticky tongue, inflating and deflating his body with air, changing his colors to various shades of green, brown, and yellow, and generally having a dull time of it. Chameleons move very slowly, so people are always capturing them and taking them home to see them turn red.[3] I'm sorry, but Chameleons do not turn the color of their surroundings as they certainly should. Their color changes are caused by light, temperature, and mood, and not by what they are on at the time. Professors who watch Chameleons to find out those things are called Chameleon watch-

---

[1] Just to show you what goes on in this world, there are more than 2,500 kinds of lizards.

[2] They belong to the *Iguanidae,* if that's any help.

[3] They do not turn red.

ers. They watch Chameleons for hours at a stretch and often change their colors much more than the Chameleons do. In bright sunlight a green Chameleon turns brown with lighter blotches. The professor turns purple with reddish spots. Little is known of the Chameleon's private life, and that is always a bad sign. It might mean anything.[4] They are also able to look in two directions at once, as their eyes act independently, and to wrap their tails around a twig.[5] Thus the Chameleon can do a number of unusual things, none of them very well and none of them worth doing. Perhaps we expect too much of the Chameleons,[6] but it's all their own fault. They started it.

---

[4] Florida Chameleons are much addicted to you know what. They have highly developed dewlaps connected with a special hyoid apparatus.

[5] The Chameleon's face reminded Aristotle of a Baboon. Aristotle wasn't much of a looker himself.

[6] If somebody gives you a Chameleon, you can always take him out in the yard for an airing. Maybe he will go away.

THE CROCODILE

We could get along very nicely without the Crocodile of the Nile. He lurks by the river's edge and grins. He is waiting to drag you under and drown you and eat you. Perhaps he thinks that is funny. You never know.[1] The Salt-water Crocodile of the Malay Peninsula is also a man-eater. The Nile Crocodile and the Salt-water Crocodile have reduced the problem of mankind to its simplest terms. They think that some specimens of mankind are a little tougher than others, and that is all there is to it. Mind you, I'm not saying they're right. The ancient Egyptians regarded the Crocodile as a sacred animal and the symbol of sunrise. This seems to have been a mistake. It was just one of the ideas people get now and then. In his spare time the Crocodile propagates his

---

[1] The Crocodile can eat under water, as his posterior nostrils, or breathing passages—that is, the Crocodile's palate—I mean he can eat under water.

kind.[2] Some people wonder whether Crocodiles have more fun in the water or on land. My guess would be both.[3] The Zic-zac, or Crocodile Bird, which flies in and out of the Crocodile's mouth crying *"Zic-zac!"* is a species of Plover. All the Plovers are a little bit crazy. The Indian Gavial of the Ganges and Brahmapootra Rivers is thirty feet long. He is the largest living reptile, which is nothing to brag of, really. He is very timid, slipping away at the sight of man. He ought to be ashamed of himself. Including the Alligators, there are nineteen kinds of Crocodilians. Eighteen would have been enough.[4]

---

[2] The mother Crocodile doesn't do anything about bringing up her young properly. She knows it's no use.

[3] Love makes the male Crocodile extremely fierce and brutal. It probably isn't the real thing.

[4] The Crocodile has been said to weep over his victims after devouring them. It wouldn't surprise me one bit if this should turn out to be true. Nothing surprises me any more.

THE ALLIGATOR

There are only two kinds of Alligators, the American and the Chinese. The Chinese Alligator has never been much of a success. He is only six feet long and he is too far away. He was discovered in 1870 by Mr. Swinhoe. The excitement has sort of died down now, but in 1870 the Chinese Alligator seemed quite important, especially to Mr. Swinhoe and the people who lived on his block. The Chinese were not at all astonished at Mr. Swinhoe's find. They had met foreigners before. The Chinese call this animal the N'Go, as they have done for centuries.[1] If you say to a Chinese, "Look here, this Alligator has teeth exactly like an Alligator and it is therefore a Chinese Alligator," he will reply, "Yes, the N'Go always has that kind of teeth and I see this N'Go has them also." There may be a comeback to that, but nobody has ever thought of it. Alligators are dumber than Crocodiles and not nearly so vicious.[2] They will hardly ever attack you unless they are cornered, and then they will generally bite off only a hand or a foot.[3] Personally, I have a little theory about what happens to people who disappear while hunting Alligators, but I'm going to keep it to myself. I don't want to worry you.[4] Alligators are more sociable than you might expect. They mate in April, May, and June. Then

---

[1] According to Chinese herpetology, the N'Go is a species of Dragon, or possibly a fish.

[2] That is the best way to tell these two animals apart, but don't let things go too far.

[3] The Florida Crocodile was regarded as fairly safe, too, until one of them knocked Dr. Ditmars down and took after him. Moral: Anything that is fairly safe will bear watching.

[4] Three million Alligators were killed in Florida between 1880 and 1900. Goody!

they just lie around killing time until the next April. Alligators go "Umph, Umph, Umph!" a good deal. We do not know the exact meaning of "Umph!" It can't be anything very important.

GALAPAGOS
1834

THE TORTOISE

Supposing I asked you to explain the difference between the Tortoise and the Turtle, what would you tell me? Oh, you *would*, eh?[1] Well, the ones that live entirely on land are Tortoises because of their terrestrial habits, and those that prefer the water are Turtles because Dr. Ditmars says so. Tortoises are slow, plodding, herbivorous, and against all modern improvements. They often live for a hundred and fifty years and what does it get them? The Giant Tortoises of the Galapagos Islands have shells over four feet long and can be ridden on if you are that fond of riding.[2] Scientists do not know where these Tortoises came from or how they got to the Galapagos Islands. In my opinion, they were there all the time. They have been almost exterminated by Cats, Dogs, Rats, Hogs, and humans.[3] In 1928 most of the Galapagos Tortoises were brought to the United States so that we could study them and watch them breed. Up to July, 1932, nothing whatever

[1] But that kind of talk isn't really scientific, is it?

[2] Darwin rode on several of them in 1834. In his account of his voyage on the *Beagle,* he states that he almost fell off several times.

[3] Mother Nature hadn't figured on us when she invented the Tortoise.

had happened and I, personally, lost interest.[4] The Greek Tortoise is a small variety subsisting mainly upon vegetation. The English buy them and put them in the garden in the belief that they eat insects. They are always wondering whatever became of the lettuces. The Gopher Tortoise of our Southern States is not worth discussing. In some quarters Tortoises are regarded as mental giants because they know their own burrows and can find their way home after prowling about. Ho, hum!

---

[4] Since that time the professors may have seen something. Let us hope so.

THE TURTLE

I don't like to criticize, but Turtles are pretty foolish. They are always making mistakes and they do not seem to learn from experience. The Leathery Turtle or Trunk-back Turtle[1] is larger than the other Sea Turtles, often weighing a thousand pounds. Naturally, he is also more foolish, as there is more of him. The Green Turtle or Soup Turtle lives in tropical waters. Sometimes he comes to New York with the Gulf Stream and all he sees is the Fulton Market. As soon as they are hatched on the beach, baby Green Turtles make straight for the water, where most of them are immediately eaten by something.[2] For a great many years the Turtle professors have been turning baby Green Turtles around to face the land, but they always turn back again and crawl to the water. I don't know what the professors expect them to do.[3] The Bastard Turtle is found only in the Atlantic Ocean.[4] He was once thought to be the offspring of the Loggerhead Turtle and the Hawksbill Turtle, but he is now regarded as perfectly all right.[5] The Box Turtle is the kind you run over on the road. He

---

[1] Or Luth.

[2] Helbigius informs us that the mother Green Turtle eats her young. Helbigius was nerts.

[3] If one of the young Turtles crawls inland some day instead of turning back to the water, what will the professors do then? What would you do?

[4] Maybe.

[5] His name might well be transferred to the Snapping Turtle—there's one for you.

has a hinge in his plastron, or lower surface, enabling him to shut himself completely inside his shell and be run over. The Mud Turtle can do this, too, but the Snapping Turtle can't, as he has a very small plastron and no hinges. So he snaps at us for fear we are going to harm the exposed parts of his lower side. The fact is, nobody gives a darn about his old lower side. The Woolworth Turtle is cute.[6]

---

[6] The Diamond-back Terrapin is almost extinct. The old-fashioned gourmet, or Terrapin inhaler, is almost extinct, too. Mother Nature tends to those things.

HOW TO BECOME EXTINCT

AND I OUGHT TO KNOW

The last two Great Auks in the world were killed June 4, 1844, on the island of Eldey, off the coast of Iceland. The last Passenger Pigeon, an old female named Martha, died September 1, 1914, peacefully, at the Cincinnati Zoo. I became extinct on August 23, 1934. I forget where I was at the time, but I shall always remember the date.

The two Great Auks were hit on the head by Jon Brandsson and Sigurdr Islefsson, a couple of Icelandic fishermen who had come from Cape Reykjanes for the purpose. A companion, Ketil Ketilsson, looked around for another Great Auk but failed to find one, naturally, since the species had just become extinct. Vilhjalmur Hakônarsson, leader of the expedition, stayed in the boat.

The main reason why these particular fishermen went birding that day is part of history. It seems that bird lovers and bird experts everywhere were upset over the disappearance of the Great Auk from its accustomed haunts and its extreme rarity even in its last refuge, the little island of Eldey. Since there was grave danger that it would soon become entirely and irrevocably extinct—as dead as the Dodo, in fact—it looked as though something would have to be done and done quickly.

Well, something was done. As always, one man rose to the occasion. Mr. Carl Siemsen, a resident of Reykjavik and quite an ornithologist on his own, hired Jon and Sigurdr and the rest of the boys to row over to Eldey and kill all the Great Auks they could find, in order that they might be properly stuffed and placed in various museums for which he acted as agent and talent scout. And of course that was one way of handling the situation. It was pretty tough on the Auks, though, wasn't it?

I don't say the museum people themselves would have hit the Great Auks on the head, or even that they would have approved such an act. I do say that ornithologists as a class, so far as I have been able to observe them, generally from a safe distance, do seem to suffer from a touch of split personality when faced with a dwindling species of bird. They appear to be torn between a sincere desire to bring that bird back to par, at any cost to themselves and to certain well-to-do persons whose names they keep in a little black book, and an uncontrollable urge or compulsion to skin a few more specimens and put them in a showcase at the earliest possible moment. I don't pretend to follow their line of reasoning, if such it may be called. To do that you have to be a Ph.D. in birdology. It takes years of hard study and I guess you have to be that way in the first place.

Right here I might offer a word of advice to the Ivory-billed Woodpecker, now the rarest bird on the North American continent and one that is going to come in for more and more attention. Keep away from bird lovers, fellows, or you'll be standing on a little wooden pedestal with a label containing your full name in Latin: *Campephilus principalis*. People will be filing past admiring your glossy blue-black feathers, your white stripes and patches, your nasal plumes in front of lores, your bright red crest and your beady yellow eyes. You'll be in the limelight, but you won't know it. I don't want to alarm you fellows, but there are only about twenty of you alive as I write these lines, and there are more than two hundred of you in American museums and in collections owned by Ivory-billed Woodpecker enthusiasts. Get it?

Yes, I know that many ornithologists are gentle, harmless souls without a murderous thought in their whole field equipment. I should like to remind them, though, that even a bird has a nervous system, and I am thinking especially of the Roseate Spoonbill, one of our few native birds with a bill shaped like a soup ladle. It can't help the Roseate Spoonbill much to go chasing over hill and dale practically twenty-four hours a day, aiming binoculars at it from behind every bush—as if it didn't know you were there!—clicking your cameras, watching every move and that sort of thing. There must be Roseate Spoonbills who haven't had a decent night's rest in years. No sleep, no nothing. And you wonder why they're neurotic.

I should like to add that the habit of climbing up into trees and rubber-stamping the eggs of birds threatened with extinction in order to warn wandering collectors away from the nests might well be abandoned in the interests of whatever remnants of sanity may still be left among our feathered friends.

Coming back to the Great Auk, if I may, I am rather surprised that I brought up the subject at all, for it is not one of my favorite birds of song or story. I lost interest some years ago when I learned that it was only as large as a tame Goose, and some say smaller—the Great Auk, mind you! When I think of the precious hours I once wasted thinking how wonderful it would be to see a Great Auk, I could sue.

Besides, it was one of those birds that lost the power of flight through long disuse of their wings, and surely that is no fault of mine, to put it no closer home. I am always a bit impatient with such birds. Under conditions prevailing in the civilized world, any bird that can't make a quick getaway is doomed, and more so if it is good to eat, if its feathers are fine for cushions, and if it makes excellent bait for Codfish when chopped into gobbets. Such a bird, to remain in the picture, must drop everything else and develop its wing muscles to the very limit. It does seem as though that should be clear even to an Auk.

Flightlessness alone, however, does not explain the fate of this species to my satisfaction, since it is a well-known fact that fish do not fly, either—that is, most fish. By the way, there are grounds for believing that the Great Auk regarded itself as more of a fish than a bird, for it made its annual migrations to Florida by water, and largely beneath the surface at that. Still and all, it didn't work out in the long run. I cannot avoid the feeling that birds migrating under water is something Mother Nature will stand just so long and no longer.

I'm afraid the Great Auks were pretty foolish in other ways, too. Like Dodos, they had a tendency to pal with just anybody. Whenever they noticed some one creeping up on them with a blunt instrument, they would rush to meet him with glad little squawks of welcome and stick out their necks. Both species did this once too often. Maybe you never heard that *doudo,* the earliest version of *Dodo,* is Portuguese for simpleton. You didn't know the Portuguese had a word for that, eh?

We should now be in a position, if we're ever going to be, to form some opinion on why the Great Auk became extinct. It would be too easy, and not very scientific, to say that it happened merely because Jon Brandsson and Sigurdr Islefsson were running amuck on the morning of June 4, 1844. But why were there only two Great Auks left on Eldey? What had been going on in this species? Just how far had *Alca impennis* evolved, whether rightly or wrongly? As Richard Swann Lull states in *Organic Evolution,* "Extinction in phylogeny has two aspects, each of which has its equivalent in ontogeny." And two aspects is putting it mildly.

Let's not be too quick to blame the human race for everything. We must remember that a great many species of animals became extinct before man ever appeared on earth. At the same time it is probably true that when two husky representatives of *Homo sapiens,* with clubs, corner the last two birds of a species, no matter how far they have or have not evolved, both the phylogeny and the ontogeny of those birds are, to all intents and purposes, over. For the present I shall have to leave it at that.

Since I mentioned two other extinct individuals in the first paragraph of this article, my readers may expect me to bring them into the story. To the best of my knowledge and belief, Martha, last of the Passenger Pigeons, is now one of the treasures of the Smithsonian Institution. After life's fitful fever she can do with a good rest. No more of those incredible, sky-darkening flights amid general uproar and pandemonium. No more dodging bullets. No more roup. Martha was far from a Squab when she left us in 1914, having reached the age of twenty-nine. Her name, by the way, is no whimsical invention of mine. She was really Martha, as anybody will tell you who knew his Cincinnati around the turn of the century.

We are not quite sure why the Passenger Pigeon became extinct as a species. Some say that all the Passenger Pigeons in the world— except Martha, presumably—were caught in a storm and perished

during their last migration southward over the Gulf of Mexico. The weakness of this theory is that Passenger Pigeons never went near the Gulf of Mexico on any pretext, let alone made a habit of flying over it in a body. I grant you there have been some bad storms over the Gulf, but that also holds true of other bodies of water.

My own view is the economic one. The food supply of these birds probably gave out, and there they were. Only the other day I came across the statement that the chief food of the Passenger Pigeon was beech-mast, a commodity which could never have been abundant enough in this country to last them forever. I never even heard of it myself except in this connection. I do think our scientists, instead of spinning picturesque yarns about the disappearance of the Passenger Pigeon, mere guesswork for the most part, might well devote themselves to the question: Whatever became of the beech-mast? Then we might get somewhere.

So much for *Ectopistes migratorius.* Nevermore, alas, will they alight in our forests by the billion, breaking down and killing the trees for miles around by the weight of their untold numbers, destroying the crops for thousands of acres in every direction, wreaking havoc and devastation upon whole counties and leaving the human population a complete wreck from shock, multiple contusions, and indigestion. People miss that sort of thing, but you needn't look for any more Passenger Pigeons. They have gone to join the Greak Auk, the Labrador Duck, the Eskimo Curlew, the Carolina Parakeet, the Heath Hen, and the Guadalupe Flicker. You won't find any of them. They're through.

What is more, sooner than we think we may see the last of the California Condor, the Everglade Kite, the Trumpeter Swan, the Whooping Crane, and the Limpkin, not to mention some of the Godwits, which haven't been doing any too well here lately. It's enough to make Donald Culross Peattie go and hang himself.

But look, Mr. Peattie, only last June a thing called a Cahow, supposed to be extinct, turned up in Bermuda as chipper as ever.

It wasn't extinct at all. Does that help any? And I honestly don't think we need worry about the Whooping Crane. There will always be people who will see to it, if it's the last thing they do, that there are plenty of Whooping Cranes around. Life has taught me that much at least.

If I may close on a personal note, I'm sorry but there seems to be some doubt whether I became extinct on August 23, 1934, or whether the date will have to be moved ahead a few years. That day was one of my birthdays and it was not my twenty-first or my thirtieth—or even, I am afraid, my fortieth. And it got me to thinking. Since then I have had more birthdays, so things haven't improved much in that respect. I find, however, that it is technically incorrect to call anybody extinct while he is still at large. I just made a mistake in one of the minor details. Some day that can be fixed in a jiffy by changing a numeral or two, and then everything will be right as rain.

Anyway, you can see how the thoughts of a person who fully believed himself to be extinct, even if he had talked himself into it, could be a bit on the somber side. Yet I had my moments, for I assure you that becoming extinct has its compensations. It's a good deal like beating the game. I would go so far as to say that becoming extinct is the perfect answer to everything and I defy anybody to think of a better. Other solutions are mere palliatives, just a bunch of loose ends, leaving the central problem untouched. But now I must snap out of all that. According to our leading scientists, I am not yet extinct, and they ought to know. Well, there's no use crying about it.

As I look back over the period since 1934, I guess I didn't go into the thing quite thoroughly enough. I never really classed myself with the Dodo, a bird we always think of as the ultimate in extinction, though I suppose the Dodo is no more extinct than anything else that is extinct, unless it's the Trilobite. Maybe I'm more like the Buffalo, which seems to be coming back now in response to no great popular demand that I can see. Did I ever tell you what happened to the Buffaloes that time? The moths got into them.

THE DINOSAUR

Long, long ago, before you and I were born, there were Dinosaurs all over the earth, except in New Zealand.[1] Dinosaurs lived and loved during the Mesozoic Era, or Age of Reptiles, which began 200,000,000 years ago and lasted until 60,000,000 years ago.[2] Then they became extinct and today there is not a single Dinosaur left, not even a small one. Some of the Dinosaurs were the largest land animals that ever lived. The Brontosaurus was seventy feet long and sixteen feet tall and weighed thirty-five tons, and his feet hurt. He was a vegetarian and perfectly harmless.[3] The Tyrannosaurus, who walked on his hind feet, was the meanest of all, as he ate the other Dinosaurs. The brain of a Dinosaur was only about the size of a nut, and some think that is why they became extinct. That can't be the reason, though, for I know plenty of animals who get by with less.[4] The Stegosaurus had a much larger secondary brain, or ganglion, in the pelvic region, so his thoughts were not on a very high plane. He didn't care what happened

---

[1] According to recent figures, mankind is from 2,000,000 to 3,000,000 years old. The earth is about 3,000,000,000 years old.

[2] There are people who know these things. Does that satisfy you?

[3] The Brontosaurus and the Diplodocus lived in Wyoming. Wyoming contains a great many fossils.

[4] The one interesting fact about the Diplodocus is that the accent is on the second syllable.

above the hips.[5] The Age of Reptiles ended because it had gone on long enough and it was all a mistake in the first place. A better day was already dawning at the close of the Mesozoic Era. There were some little warm-blooded animals around which had been stealing and eating the eggs of the Dinosaurs, and they were gradually learning to steal other things, too.[6] Civilization was just around the corner.[7]

---

[5] The animal mind was not perfected until the Pleistocene Period, when it developed the ability to worry.

[6] This kind of progress is called evolution.

[7] Dinosaur eggs are expensive nowadays, costing several thousand dollars apiece, but each one is guaranteed to be millions of years old. You could club together and get one.

THE PLESIOSAUR

There were no real Sea Serpents in the Mesozoic Era, but the Plesiosaurs were the next thing to it. The Plesiosaurs were reptiles who had gone back to the water because it seemed like a good idea at the time. As they knew little or nothing about swimming, they rowed themselves around in the water with their four paddles, instead of using their tails for propulsion like the brighter marine animals.[1] This made them too slow to catch fish, so they kept adding vertebrae to their necks until their necks were longer than all the rest of their body. Then they would dart their heads at the fish from a distance of twenty-five or thirty feet.[2] Thus the Plesiosaurs resembled the modern Sea Serpent above the water-line, though they were almost a total loss farther down. They might have had a useful career as Sea Serpents, but they were before their time. There was nobody to scare except fish, and that was hardly worth while. Their heart was not in the work. As they were made so poorly, Plesiosaurs had very little fun. They had to go ashore to lay their eggs and that sort of thing.[3] They also tried to get along with gizzards instead of stomachs, swallowing pebbles after each

---

[1] Such as the Ichthyosaurs, who used their paddles for balancing and steering. The Plesiosaurs did everything wrong.

[2] They got the fish, but it would have been much simpler to learn the Australian crawl.

[3] The Ichthyosaurs stayed right in the water and gave birth to living young. It can be done if you know how.

meal to grind their food. At least, pebbles have been found near fossil Plesiosaurs, and to a scientist that means the Plesiosaur had a gizzard.[4] During the Cretaceous Period many of the inland seas dried up, leaving the Plesiosaurs stranded without any fish.[5] Just about that time Mother Nature scrapped the whole Age of Reptiles and called for a new deal. And you see what she got.

---

[4] This is Gimmick's Law.

[5] Here we see the working of another Law of Nature: No water, no fish.

THE PTERODACTYL

Life was very difficult for the average reptile in the Mesozoic Era, what with the Dinosaurs and the humidity, so some of them took to the air to get away from it all. The Pterodactyls grew leathery wings attached to their outer digits and hind legs, which enabled them to fly in a clumsy sort of way.[1] They tumbled through the air more or less as Bats do today, and they were never quite sure where they were going to light.[2] They were even worse off on land, as they were constantly tripping over their wings, involved as these were with the wrong parts of their body. The Rhamphorhynchus, an early Pterodactyl, had pointed jaws full of teeth, a long tail with a membranous tip, and a somewhat half-witted expression. The Rhamphorhynchus could never have become popular, if only because of his name. Lots of people wouldn't get it. The Pteranodon, a much larger Pterodactyl, lived in Kansas in the Cretaceous Period. He had no teeth and no tail and may be regarded as an improvement.[3] He also had a birdlike beak and a bony crest almost two feet long on the back of his skull

---

[1] In those days animals thought nothing of growing a new limb or organ to adapt themselves to conditions. We seem to have lost the knack.

[2] Some scientists say the Pterodactyls merely glided and never attained true flight. As a matter of fact, they flew.

[3] If you call the lack of one's teeth and tail an improvement.

which gave him a rather topheavy look. We do not know exactly what this thing was for, but the Pteranodon probably knew. It was clever of the Pterodactyls to think of flying, but that's all you can say for them. They were doomed from the start because they had no feathers and no wishbone, or furcula, as flying vertebrates should have. Pretty soon the Archaeopteryx, a genuine bird, came along, and the Pterodactyls faded away. They didn't belong in the picture and public opinion was against them.[4] The Archaeopteryx was not much of a bird, but at least it had feathers. As for the Pterodactyls, the best thing to do is just to forget them.[5]

---

[4] If you're booked for extinction, there's nothing much you can do about it.

[5] Bats are going to flop, too, and everybody knows it except the Bats themselves. Well, that's always the way.

THE WOOLLY MAMMOTH

The Woolly Mammoth is awfully disappointing when you get to know him. We were all brought up to believe that the Woolly Mammoth was three or four times as large as the Circus Elephant, as he certainly should have been. But now they tell us he was no such thing. He was only nine or ten feet in height, or about the size of the ordinary Indian Elephant, and not as big as the African Elephant.[1] It seems the name of the Woolly Mammoth was derived from the Tartar word *mama,* meaning earth, as the Tartars believed that he lived underground and burrowed through the soil.[2] So it is our own fault if we drew the wrong conclusions and thought of the Mammoth as perfectly immense. Perhaps the Woolly Mammoths could have done better if they had tried harder. They lived in Europe, Asia, and North America during the Glacial Period, or Ice Age, when a cold spell would last for thousands of years at a time.[3] They were covered with a thick coat of reddish-brown wool and they also had long black hair. They were prepared for any amount of cold, yet they all disappeared

---

[1] The Imperial Mammoths were a little larger, but they had no wool, and there were only a few of them. They never caught on, somehow.

[2] But it seems the Tartars have no such word as *mama* in their language. That doesn't clear things up much, does it?

[3] The animals of the Ice Age got used to this. They never expected any decent weather, as we sometimes do.

about 20,000 years ago. Some say they died of the heat when the weather cleared up, and others say they fell through cracks in the ice. We do not really know why the Woolly Mammoth became extinct. Early Man killed some of them, of course. But most of the time Early Man stayed right in his cave, holding hands with Early Woman. I wouldn't know what the Woolly Mammoth did about that sort of thing. Not nearly enough, I suspect.

THE GIANT GROUND SLOTH

The Giant Ground Sloth or Megatherium of the Pleistocene Period was too much of the same thing. He was eighteen or twenty feet long, and that is a lot of anything, let alone a Ground Sloth. Ground Sloths originated in South America, but they have also been found in this country, I'm sorry to say.[1] The Ground Sloth hadn't much personality of his own. He was more like three other animals. He had the head of a Tree Sloth and the legs and tail of an Anteater and he also looked like a Bear.[2] The demand for this particular combination gradually grew smaller, once the novelty had worn off, and the Ground Sloth was left holding the bag. Some of them lived on until a few thousand years ago, but they never came back.[3] Science teaches us that highly specialized animals tend to become extinct, as they cannot adapt themselves to changing conditions. The Ground Sloth specialized in laziness. He would sit under a tree and think until he was hungry. Then he

---

[1] Thomas Jefferson once lectured about the bones of a Ground Sloth found in Virginia. It was a fine speech, with some ringing tributes to the king of beasts, for Mr. Jefferson thought the bones were those of an extinct Lion.

[2] The Moropus of the Miocene Period tried to be a Horse, a Tapir, and a Rhinoceros all at the same time. As he discovered, it can't be done.

[3] The Patagonians are said to have domesticated the Ground Sloth. The Patagonians are now extinct.

would pull down the branches, eat all the leaves, and move on to the next one. He also took naps in the afternoon.[4] The Ground Sloth did not reproduce very often because it was too much trouble. Even if he wanted to do something very much, he was too lazy to do it, and that is always the beginning of the end. After a while such animals get so that they don't even want to do it. They are then practically extinct. So now we have only two kinds of Sloths, the Ai and the Unau. Two is plenty.

---

[4] He could not see the advantage of staying awake in the daytime. By the way, what *is* the advantage?

THE DODO

The Dodo never had a chance. He seems to have been invented for the sole purpose of becoming extinct and that was all he was good for. I'm not blaming the Dodo, but he was just a mess. For one thing, his appearance was against him. He was a member of the Pigeon tribe, about the size of a Swan. He had an ugly face with a large hooked beak, a tail in the wrong place, wings too small and weak for flight, and a very prominent stomach. You can't look like that and survive. Or can you?[1] Up to 1505 the Dodos had everything their own way on the island of Mauritius in the Indian Ocean, and the future looked rosy, indeed. They probably thought they were making splendid progress as a species and had most of life's problems licked. And then came the Portuguese.[2] The Portuguese called the birds *doudos,* or fools, because they would associate with the Portuguese on friendly terms and allow themselves to be hit on the head with clubs. The Portuguese finally got tired of this and left, and the Dutch arrived in 1598 with a shipload of Pigs, Dogs, and Cats, showing that if it isn't one thing it's

---

[1] The Dodo's carina, a part of the sternum, was rudimentary. If not used rather constantly, the carina will atrophy or even disappear altogether. Some birds don't know that.

[2] Here's a little slogan you may find helpful most any time: Look out for the Portuguese!

another. The Dutch ate the grownup Dodos and the other animals ate the eggs and the young, and by 1691 there was not a single Dodo left on earth. By 1755 there was not even a stuffed one in a museum, for the museum people had thrown them out. Today any museum will pay you a fortune for a stuffed Dodo, if you can find one.[3] Little is known of the Dodo's daily life and I'd rather not think about it. They were probably monogamous, at least they give one that impression.[4] Most of us feel that we could never become extinct. The Dodo felt that way, too.

---

[3] I'd be willing to bet that there are several stuffed Dodos somewhere in the British Museum, if they'd only look more carefully. There must be.

[4] Still, they were Pigeons, and there is nothing slow about a Pigeon. Quite the contrary.

APPENDIX

ARE THE INSECTS WINNING?

Whatever you may have heard, I am not a chronic worrier about the Insect Menace. I'm not even sure I believe in the thing, certainly not in its worst form. That is, I don't believe, as some of our scientists do, that the insects are going to wipe us humans off the map eventually, take full possession of the globe, and establish what has been named, a little too horribly for my taste, the Insect Age.

Frankly, if I took that for gospel, I would be thoroughly upset. I'd probably be on my way to the South Pole, or somewhere. I wouldn't be sitting here with a lot of statistics, calmly marshaling my arguments for and against the prospects of an Insect Age—an occupation I must stop, by the way, if I'm ever to get anything else done. I mean I'm not worried, exactly. I want to find out.

I can't see that I have an insect phobia just because I sometimes bring insects into the conversation and ask a few questions, without, I may say, very satisfactory results. "Oh, yes," is a typical answer I get. "Of course the next age after the Age of Man will be the Insect Age. I thought everybody knew that!" A gayer soul will perhaps add, "Why certainly! Look around you, man—can't you see where we're headed?" Then he'll go on about his business as though he had said nothing at all out of the ordinary, nothing in the least appalling. I can't help admiring that kind of people, if only for their spirit.

One must fight these things out by oneself, I suppose. Even the

professors who predict the Insect Age and issue warnings about it
are not much help. They never give us the details. They leave vast
practical problems untouched. For instance, if the insects do win
and set up a government, how will they manage, without us to
raise crops for them? Do they intend to exterminate mankind, or
will they let a few of us remain in some minor capacity, such as
planting apple trees for the Codling Moth and cotton for the
Boll Weevil?

And which particular orders, families, genera, and species of the
Class *Insecta* are going to do whatever it is they are going to do?
Since it is hardly conceivable that any new and more frightful
insect will emerge at this late date—or have I just talked myself
into that?—the scientists doubtless have in mind the regular run
of destructive farm pests that we read about in the papers. These
insects constitute a menace in the here and now, but I happen to
have in my possession some bulletins from the Department of
Agriculture indicating, at least to me, that they are all likely to
find themselves at a loose end before long, let alone conquering
mankind. Try to imagine the San José Scale running things. You
can't.

As I understand it, the Hessian Fly, the European Corn-borer,
and the whole lot of them, even the Boll Weevil, are on the tobog-
gan right now. Though we have not beaten them yet, it seems we
have succeeded in outguessing them from season to season by
rotating our crops, or something of the sort, and we have more
plans in the making. Let me add that if outguessing a Boll Weevil
strikes you as nothing for an adult human being to boast of, you
try it some time. And look what we did to the Mediterranean
Fruit-fly!

As for the less publicized insects, unless I willfully misread the
evidence, the Western Grasshopper, or Rocky Mountain Locust,
hasn't been itself, really, since 1876, when it devoured Kansas and
Iowa and parts of Nebraska, Texas, Oklahoma, and Missouri. I
will say for the Grasshopper that after it has eaten up all there is
to eat it goes away and lets you alone for a while. And the Clover-
seed Midge (*Dasyneura leguminicola* Lintner) appears to have
given up any hopes it may have had of becoming dominant even
in its own family, the *Cecidomyidae*. It should never have tried.

Much the same can be said of the Thrips, those tiny plant
insects that haven't so much as a decent singular to their name, if

one wished to specify an individual Thrips. You may speak of many Thrips, or of one Thrips, but never of one Thrip, however strongly you may feel that such a ruling is in restraint of your personal liberties. Nor may you employ the word *Thripses* to mean one or more Thrips, convenient as it might be in a pinch. *The New English Dictionary* states, with what end in view I don't know, unless to give its readers a false sense of security—and if so, it failed in my case—that the analogical English plural of *Thrips* would be *Thripses,* but what good is that if you mustn't say it? As our language develops, the word *Thripses,* to indicate more than one Thrips, may fall naturally enough into our common speech. I fancy that whoever used it now would do so at the risk of looking pretty analogical.

The Thrips are still at it, blighting the leaves and blossoms of lots of plants, yet I am satisfied in my own mind that if mankind is to go down in defeat before an insect, it won't be a Thrips. We seldom hear of serious outbreaks any more, partly because most people nowadays wouldn't know a Thrips if they saw one and therefore would not report it to the proper authorities. Besides, some Thrips are only one-fiftieth of an inch long and very hard to see unless one is specially organized and equipped for the purpose. The result is that plenty of amateur gardeners sit around and watch a favorite cineraria wither and waste away without ever suspecting the real cause. They just think the plant has withered.

Out in Westchester, once a paradise for Thrips, conditions seem to have improved. At any rate, that man in Pelham Manor has been writing fewer and fewer letters to the papers of late years about the Thrips in his backyard, and no news from that fellow is good news. Or it may mean that the Thrips in his backyard are worse. They may have increased to such an extent as to preclude the writing of letters to the papers or any other activity beyond spraying them with whale-oil soap, nicotine sulphate, kerosene emulsion, pyrethrum, Paris green, O. K. Thrips Killer, or whatever the poor man prefers. Well, it's not my funeral.

My readers will hardly expect me to take up all the existing insects in this article, as about 750,000 species have already been described by science and there may be as many as ten million other kinds at large, including the red-eyed, green-whiskered thing that flew into my bedroom one night, buzzed slowly twice around the reading-lamp, and then flew out again, probably on its way back to hell. I'd rather not say any more about that. There's nothing to say, is there?

I must mention, however, that the Department of Agriculture has its eye on those abysmal little animals that prey on strawberries, and that something will be done. Indeed, something must be done, if it takes our whole available supply of arsenate of lead,

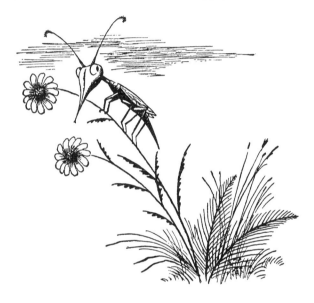

and I, for one, can think of no better use to which all that arsenate of lead could be put. For some reason I have never been able to fathom, the public is not sufficiently aroused about these strawberry demons. A man said to me only the other day, "Well, you can't blame them." That isn't the right attitude, with things the way they are.

To end on a more cheerful note, I think I have found a fallacy or two in some of the more spectacular arguments used by the Insect Age enthusiasts when they are hardest pressed. For one thing, the fact that insects as a class are 300,000,000 years old, if it is a fact, while we have been here only about 1,000,000 years, or 3,000,000 at the outside, does not prove to me that the insects are bound to win. It takes more than mere old age to get along these days. I think it quite likely that the insects themselves would be surprised to hear of their supposed dreams of glory after 300,000,000 years of being slapped around, swatted, and stepped on by all the other animals. By now, surely, their spirit must be pretty well broken.

We are told, furthermore, that nine-tenths of all the creatures on earth today are insects. That is an effective, not to say a rather frightful bit of statistics until one lives with it for a while and comes to realize that it doesn't mean, as it seems to mean at first glance, that nine-tenths of all the creatures on earth today are Bengal Tigers. Nor am I sold on the frequently repeated statement that insects, take them by and large, are by far the most successful form of terrestrial animals. To that I say yes, if you call that success.

Anyway, I intend to quit arguing with entomologists for the rest of the current year. I never convince them, and they aren't doing me any good. I have an answer all ready for the next entomologist who draws me aside and informs me in hollow tones that the insects are gaining. I shall yawn slightly and reply, "Well, they may be, on some people." That will be just whistling in the dark, maybe, but it ought to stop him.

THOUGHTS ON THE ERMINE

I am often asked whether the Stoat, or Ermine, is monogamous. I really don't know. And I can't see that it matters. My guess would be that a good deal depends upon the individual Stoat, or Ermine.

A more worth-while question, as questions go about the Stoat, or Ermine, is this one: Why does the Stoat, which is brown in summer, turn white in winter, thus becoming an Ermine? For that is what happens, within certain limits, and allowing for climate, whim, and those things.

I'm afraid we have been a little too sure that the Stoat turns white to make itself invisible against its background of snow, in accordance with the theory of protective coloration. That explanation is very pretty and snug, but it looks silly sometimes, especially when there is no snow within miles. Perhaps we need more data on whether the Stoat was expecting snow when it turned white.

And when there is plenty of snow, as in the Arctic, Ermines have a habit of finding and racing around on bare, wind-swept spots where they are much more conspicuous than they ever were when they were Stoats. They act, in a word, as though they had never heard of the theory of protective coloration and would not care if they had. I should not be surprised if Ermines want to be as conspicuous as possible and are miserable when they are not.

Even assuming that some Ermines may remain constantly on snow, as called for by our theory, their whereabouts would still be an open secret to all concerned because of the black tips on their tails. They would melt into the Arctic background only if the snow were sprinkled with small lumps of coal, which snow in its natural state is not. Besides, Ermines are not at all the color of snow, but sort of yellowish. They have to be bleached.

In actual practice, nobody in the Arctic has any difficulty in spotting Ermines at a considerable distance, as Ermine-hunters have long been aware. An Ermine-hunter who held Ermines to be invisible would be regarded by his fellows as decidedly eccentric and would not succeed in life.

Nor does the Ermine seem to deceive its own prey, the Arctic Ptarmigan, which is in its turn provided with white feathers in order—so they say—to render itself invisible to the Ermine. Theoretically, the Ptarmigan believes that what is creeping up on it is a piece of snow, and the Ermine is after something it can't see but wants to eat. Who do they think they're fooling, anyway? Just a few old professors?

Those of us who have lost faith in this concealing business may, if we wish, swallow the rival theory that the Stoat turns white to keep warm. A recent supporter of this view mentions as proof what he calls the well-known fact that white fur is much better for conserving the animal heat than brown or black fur. Since when is this a well-known fact, and to whom?

I don't feel that I've got to the bottom of this warmth theory yet, so I'm not saying all I think. I will say, however, that a black animal always looks warmer to me than a white one, and I shall never be able to feel otherwise. It would be hard to convince me, for instance, that a Polar Bear on a cake of ice is ever really warm. It may be fairly warm, in spots, but I believe it would be more comfortable in black, and that goes for Ermines, too.

Moreover, if I had to keep warm by conserving my animal heat with fur or feathers, I should insist upon black, science or no science. I should probably freeze, too, since I appear to have no animal heat from about October to the last of March, and am obliged to use a rather complicated system of electric heaters, over and above any arrangements my landlord may have made. I fear it would be all up with me if I were forced to rely on such heat as I, personally, can muster during the colder months.

Still, I have an unpleasant feeling that the warmth man may have known what he was talking about. I have tried to go into it with dozens of people, and I always get exactly the same statement: "Well, we wear white clothing in the summer to keep cool because white reflects the sun's rays." About half of them add a few remarks on costume among the Bedouins, leaving quite a gap to be bridged, if you ask me. Or perhaps there is some subtle relationship between Ermines and Bedouins that I don't grasp.

Now, supposing that white clothing does reflect the sun's rays, and supposing it also conserves the animal heat, then how is a Bedouin better off in white clothing than in black, or does the animal heat, of which Bedouins have a lot, get through the seams and around the edges in some manner that is impossible with fur? That is the kind of thoughts I've been having lately. It won't do.

I have also met several persons who say Stoats turn into Ermines so that ladies can have Ermine coats. That is the worst guess of all, for Stoats are among the meanest little varmints in creation. They would probably go out of their way to prevent ladies from having Ermine coats if they could.

And right there, strangely enough, is an idea. Maybe Stoats turn into Ermines simply because they can't help it. That's my theory until further notice, or at least until I rest up from the other theories.

814.54 C921h 1983

Cuppy, Will, 1884-1949.

How to become extinct